Finding Hank

The Most-Often Asked Questions About Hank the Cowdog

HANK THE COWDOG®

by John R. Erickson

Illustrations by Gerald L. Holmes

Maverick Books, Inc.

MAVERICK BOOKS, INC.
Published by Maverick Books, Inc.
P.O. Box 549, Perryton, TX 79070
Phone: 806.435.7611
www.hankthecowdog.com

First published in the United States of America by Maverick Books, Inc. 2019.

1 3 5 7 9 10 8 6 4 2

Library of Congress Control Number: 2019945760

ISBN: 978-1-59188-999-1

Cover art by Gerald L. Holmes

Designed & Published in the United States of America
Printed in China

Dedicated to Kristine Erickson

John R. Erickson

Slim Chance

". . . the best family entertainment in years." – *USA Today*

"The Lone Star State's best-known canine." – *The Houston Chronicle*

"...Most of us on the American-Statesman web desk grew up avidly reading the "Hank" books...The iconic children's series, written by Texas author John R. Erickson, turns 35 this year. With a 70th book on the way in September, there's no stopping this crime-fighting ranch dog." – *The Austin American-Statesman*

"The best-selling Hank the Cowdog children's book series [is] about a smelly but lovable cowdog that lives on a Panhandle ranch..." – *Texas Monthly*

"For the detectin' and protectin' exploits of the canine Mike Hammer, hang Hank's name right up there with those of other anthropomorphic greats...But there's no sentimentality in Hank: he's just plain more rip-roaring fun than the others. Hank's misadventures as head of ranch security on a spread somewhere in the Texas Panhandle are marvelous situation comedy." – *School Library Journal*

"Knee-slapping funny and gets kids reading." – *Fort Worth Star-Telegram*

"Hank is the self-proclaimed head of security on a ranch, a canine Inspector Clouseau with a penchant for creative wordsmithing as he narrates his misadventures. "Hank the Cowdog has never aspired to ordinarity," Hank once said. Three decades after the dog's debut, there are more than 60 Hank books and a couple of dozen other books from Erickson." – *The Dallas Morning News*

"A mixture of true-life experiences, comedy, and adventure."
– *Little Rock Arkansas Gazette*

"Full of regional humor . . . vocals are suitably poignant and ridiculous. A wonderful yarn." – *Booklist*

Part Four: Stage and Studio

Part Five: Personal Questions

JRE with his Arabian mare, Nocona. Western Horseman photo.

PREFACE

Over the years, I have done hundreds of author visits in schools and have read my stories aloud to audiences from Key West, Florida, to Fairbanks, Alaska. In every program, I leave fifteen minutes at the end so the audience can ask questions.

I also receive a large volume of mail from fans—emails to the Hank website, letters written on scraps of paper, Christmas cards, birthday cards, and sometimes a packet of letters from an entire class—and each letter might contain four or five questions. Some express curiosity about me or the process of writing, but they all focus on the same theme: Hank the Cowdog.

Hank has become a popular fellow. We have sold over nine million books about his adventures, and we are now hearing from second and third generation Hank fans. They, too, are curious. They want to know…who is Hank? Where did he come from and how did all of this come about?

In Q&A sessions and in replies to fan letters, I'm not able to address those questions in the manner they deserve because the answers are not always short or simple. They require a bigger canvas and that is the purpose of this book. I'm going to pose some of the questions I've been asked over the years and answer them in a detailed manner.

For the convenience of readers who might be working on a class project, or who might not be interested in every topic, I've provided a list of questions at the beginning, and have divided them into categories:

1. Early Years
2. Writing
3. Characters and Settings
4. Stage and Studio
5. Personal Questions

You can pick and choose your topics and use the book as a Hank Encyclopedia, if you wish, or start at the beginning and read it straight through. I've tried to make it as pleasant and readable as possible.

I would like to express my appreciation to those people who allowed us to use their photographs, especially Chason Laing and his company Lumindeo for letting us use still shots from a documentary film he made in 2015. Readers can view the entire film on the Lumindeo website.

I also owe an enormous debt of gratitude to the people who have worked beside Kris and me over the years: Gary and Kim Rinker, Gerald and Carol Holmes, Trev Tevis, Janee McCartor, Jody Morris, Jane Friesen, Linda McDowell, Carol Sell, Debbie Williford, Carlos Casso, Mark Erickson, and the lady who designed this handsome book, Nikki Georgacakis Earley.

I apologize for talking so much about myself in these pages. I understand that I merely work for the dog and that readers are more interested in Hank than me, but I can't think of a way of answering the questions without involving myself. Sorry.

jre

Part One

The Early Years

Perryton, Texas – photos courtesy of the Museum of the Plains

Front: Ellen Erickson. Middle Row: Great-grandmother Perlina Sherman, Anna Beth Erickson with John squirming in her arms, Aunt Bennett Harter, Grandmother Mabel Sherman Curry, Charles Erickson. Back row: Sergeant Joe Erickson, great-uncle Roy Sherman. Taken in Seminole, Texas, 1945.

- PART ONE -

What was it like, growing up in Perryton?

Not long ago, I drove down the street where I grew up, the eleven-hundred block of Amherst in Perryton, Texas. The houses seemed smaller than I remembered, and most showed their age, but I recognized them all and recalled the names of the boys who lived in them: Robert O'Rear, Lefty Mayberry, Bob Wright, Harry and Grant Drake, Jimmy Gipson, Jim Bruce Johnson, Bobby Barnett, and the Symons twins, Kerry and Terry.

I saw no children playing in my old neighborhood. Perhaps they were inside, watching television or texting on their phones. Back in the Fifties, the boys on our block would have been outside, playing football on a vacant lot, climbing trees, playing with our dogs and cats, or digging a "hideout" in someone's back yard.

We occupied a world that had no daycare centers, no sports leagues, and no shopping malls. We invented our own entertainment, created our own facilities for football, basketball, volleyball, and track — coached, refereed, and played the games ourselves.

In the Fifties, Perryton had a population of about three thousand, and a fairly stable, sometimes-prosperous economy based on wheat farming and cattle ranching. The discovery of oil and natural gas in 1956 brought new people into the community and took some of the sting out of the drought of the Fifties.

The Perryton of my youth was a good place to grow up, and whatever problems I encountered as a boy were not significant. I worried that I might be too skinny to excel in football, and was self-conscious that I had to start wearing glasses in the third grade.

I was ashamed that we lived in an old house and drove old cars. My father was shrewd enough to understand that the purchase of a new automobile was a poor investment, since it lost twenty or thirty percent of its value the moment you drove it away from the dealership.

He was right about that, but it did nothing to ease the embarrassment I felt, riding down Main Street in our old yellow 1954 Plymouth.

The Erickson home in Perryton. John and his dog Frisky occupied the bedroom on the second floor.

My heroes in those days were an odd mix: ranchers and cowboys from my mother's family; characters from the Bible (Moses, David, Samson, and Samuel); and figures from Texas history (Houston, Bowie, Travis, and Crockett), with an occasional name from current events (Douglas McArthur and Dwight Eisenhower).

As to the future, I gave it little thought. At various times in my youth, I considered being a surgeon, lawyer, rancher, minister, and politician. The thought of becoming a writer never entered my mind until I was a senior in high school.

Church. Church attendance was probably the most important element in the life of my family. We belonged to the First Baptist Church because that was the church my mother had grown up in (my father had been raised Presbyterian in Independence, Missouri), and when the church doors opened, the Ericksons were there.

Preparation for Sunday services began on Saturday night when we polished our shoes, laid out our Sunday-best clothes, and studied the Sunday school lesson, which included memorizing a Bible verse. At nine-thirty on the Sabbath, we were there for Sunday school. At 10:45, we moved up to the sanctuary for a service of preaching and hymn singing. At 6:30 we returned to the church for Training Union and evening services.

When we arrived at the Sunday school classroom, we were given an envelope to fill out. It had check-boxes for attendance, tithe (usually a dime or quarter that we sealed inside the envelope), memory verse, and lesson prepared. The church kept records and gave an award at the end of the year for perfect attendance. The first year's award was a pin we could wear on our lapel, and subsequent years' awards were bars that fastened onto the first pin. By the time I reached high school, I had eight years of perfect attendance.

Those Baptist Sunday school classes were places where actual education occurred. Our teachers came prepared, and we were drilled on the Bible. We learned verses and memorized all the books in the Old and New Testaments. We sang in choirs, acted in Christmas plays, and did some of our first reading in a book that is still difficult for me, the King James Bible.

Grandfather Buck Curry holding Aunt Bennett, with Roy Sherman.

We always suspected that the kids in the Methodist Church across the street were having more fun than we were, but we got a solid foundation in biblical studies, which included history, literature, grammar, manners, and morals.

My family bought our Sunday clothes at Castles Dry Goods Store on Main Street. Both Virgil Castle and his wife served as my Sunday school teachers, as did Brother Marvin Montgomery who worked in the store after he finished his farming in the fall. One of the certainties of life during the Fifties was that our new clothes would carry the scent of Mr. Castle's cigars. He smoked them all the time.

I once told his daughter-in-law, Rita, that until I went off to college, I thought a new suit of clothes was supposed to smell like a King Edward cigar.

Television. I first saw a television set in 1954, when Bob Wright's parents purchased one of the first to appear in our town. To get a signal from one of the TV stations in Amarillo, 120 miles away, they had to erect a fifty-foot tower with an antenna on the top. Even with the tower, the signal was often so poor that the screen was clouded by what we referred to as "snow."

Cable television came to Perryton in 1957, bringing a better signal (still black-and-white, no color), and many families signed up for the service. My father didn't like television and kept it out of our home until 1958, when his brother gave us an old black-and-white TV set. I think Uncle Carl worried that, without television, our family was becoming unnormal.

Joe Erickson didn't mind being unnormal and kept the TV in a closet for months. When he finally brought it out, it was as though he had allowed a rattlesnake to move into our home. After a few years, he softened a bit. I know he enjoyed watching the Kennedy-Nixon debates, and I have a few memories of our family watching the variety shows of Ed Sullivan and Steve Allen. I think he actually liked Steve Allen. Even television couldn't conceal that he was an intelligent man and a gifted pianist.

In spite of Joe Erickson's admiration for Steve Allen, there was never any doubt that he regarded television as an alien force. When he was in the house, I either turned it off or watched my programs with feelings of guilt, knowing that he thought I was wasting hours of my life.

What programs did I watch? "Victory At Sea," "Gunsmoke," "Dragnet," "Howdy Doodie," "Roy Rogers," "Jungle Jim," "Walt Disney," and "The Little Rascals." I remember watching the Cotton Bowl game at Bob Wright's house in 1956 or 1957. A Perryton boy, Don Cooper, was a starting tackle for TCU and captain of the team. Today, Don and I attend the same church in Perryton. Recently, at a church luncheon, he told me that in college, he played against Bart Star and Jimmy Brown. He didn't play with Bob Lilly at TCU but knew him.

Television in those days was rather innocent, but that has changed a lot. My father would be pleased that Kris and I don't have television and raised three kids without it.

Movies. Hollywood movies were a potent force in our daily lives, and kids in my neighborhood often walked a mile to the center of town to attend the Saturday matinee. A dime got us into the Ellis Theater, and another nickel bought Milk Duds, popcorn, or licorice.

Sometimes the whole family attended a movie during the week. Among the movies I remember seeing were "Singing In the Rain," "Gone With the Wind," "The Robe," "Bambi," and "Peter Pan." I sat with my sister Ellen during "Bambi" and she cried at the end.

The latest movie to appear at the Ellis Theater often set the tone for our outside activities the following week. A Civil War movie caused us to divide up into Yankees and Rebels. A pirate film inspired us to fashion swords out of curtain rods and fence pickets, and to transform ragged Chinese elm trees into three-masted ships, with sails made of our mothers' sheets.

We played Alamo, knights in shining armor, Davy Crockett, cowboys and Indians, and daredevil (I still carry scars from bicycle wrecks), but our favorite and most passionate movie recreations involved World War II, which was still a vivid memory in our community. For weeks after a WWII movie came to town, we stormed the beaches of Iwo Jima and Normandy, pelting each other with dirt clods or tomatoes from our mothers' gardens.

Audie Murphy was our favorite actor. Not only had he won the Congressional Medal of Honor in combat, but he had cousins in Perryton and had spent summers working in the local wheat harvest.

Most of our fathers had served in the military and had brought home relics that we put to use. At the age of ten, I went into backyard combat wearing my father's wool army jacket with sergeant stripes, and endured great discomfort to wear his steel helmet (without the inside liner). It was a bit like walking around with a cast iron pot on my head. Wearing the helmet caused pain, but it was pain with a purpose.

Radio. Radio was an important source of entertainment and news for us, and my memories of that medium probably go back to 1948 or 1949. Radios in the late 1940s and early 1950s were large devices, composed of an array of wires and glass tubes. Our radio occupied a standup cabinet that would have required two strong men to lift, and it stood near the center of our living room, beside my father's Baldwin grand piano.

As a family, we listened to the evening news, delivered by Gabriel Heeter and Fulton Lewis, Jr. I remember hearing that the Soviets had exploded their first atomic bomb and that President Truman had relieved General Douglas

McArthur of his command. The former was a source of anxiety, and the second gave my family another reason for not liking President Truman.

General McArthur was considered a hero in our home. President Truman was not so highly esteemed, although I'm not sure why. Perhaps my parents were solid Republicans by then. When General Eisenhower ran for president, I went to school wearing a lapel button that said "I Like Ike."

In the afternoons after school, I often listened to radio programs: Sergeant Preston of the Yukon, Skye King, and Bobby Benson and the B Bar B Riders. Evenings brought "The Shadow" and a series called "I Love a Mystery." Our whole family sat around the radio to hear an evening program, "Family Theater," which always opened with the same line: "More things are wrought by prayer than this world dreams of."

One of the most popular daytime programs in our area came from our local station, KEYE: "The All-Request Hour." Coy Thompson and Gus Hinshaw played popular tunes of the day, gave local news, weather, and birthday greetings, and chatted with listeners who called in.

The music was a mix of country, gospel/inspirational, and Top Forty hits: The Sons of the Pioneers, Spike Jones and the City Slickers, Patty Page, Tennessee Ernie Ford, Ernest Tubb, Hank Williams, Bing Crosby, and Bob Wills. The Weavers had several tunes on the Top Forty, "On Top of Old Smokey" and "Irene, Goodnight."

One consequence of my growing up as a radio kid is that I have never felt comfortable with television. Radio allows some distance between the medium and the listener, and in that space, listeners can fill in the pictures with their own imagination. I prefer it that way. Television is more possessive and takes over that space with its rapid flashing images. I like my pictures better than theirs.

You might have noticed that television is never mentioned in the Hank books. Little Alfred doesn't spend his time watching television. He plays outside with his dogs and toy trucks, as I did, and Slim Chance gets his news and weather reports from a radio, as I still do.

Did you have a dog?

One day in 1955, Bob Wright and I were hiking across the vacant fields near our homes in Perryton and encountered a smallish brown, short-haired mutt of a dog. He had a ringworm on his neck, wore no collar, and followed me home. I asked Mother if I could keep him and she said yes. We called him Frisky.

Mother had never allowed any of her three children to keep pets inside the house, but she made an exception with Frisky. Maybe I begged, or maybe Frisky just won her heart. I think she detected a melancholy side to my nature and her instincts told her that I needed the companionship of a dog.

Frisky and I became inseparable friends. When I came home from school every afternoon, he was there in the yard, waiting for me. We played and hiked together. I dressed him up in clothes and told him stories. Sometimes, on long winter evenings when Mother was late getting supper on the table, Frisky and I shared spooned portions of Dash dog food out in the back yard.

Mother would have been horrified, had she known I was eating dog food, but

John R. Erickson age 3 in Midland, Texas.

it really wasn't bad. A famous brand of canned chili, which I won't name, tastes much the same to me. I don't mean that as an insult to the chili, but to say that Dash dog food was pretty good, if a guy was hungry enough.

Frisky and I shared a bedroom on the second floor of our old house on Amherst. On cold winter nights, when the Panhandle wind rattled the wood-framed windows, we burrowed under the covers and kept each other warm.

When Frisky and I were alone, I talked to him, just as though he were a person, and felt that he understood and "talked" back with his eyes, ears, and tail. I had no way of knowing that this would show up decades later as "research" for a series of novels narrated by a dog. The Hank stories reflect the experience of an author who has spent a great deal of time in the company of dogs.

Over the years, I've had other dogs who became dear friends—Spike, Foxie, Poochie, Sophie, Texie, Tango, Dixie, Daisy, Rosie, and others whose names have faded from memory—but Frisky was the dog who shared my childhood.

Were you a reader?

In an interview, Larry McMurtry said that he grew up in a home that had no books or magazines. That is hard for me to imagine. Both my parents felt a reverence for the written word. They subscribed to a number of magazines (*Reader's Digest, Time, Life, National Geographic, Boy's Life, The Baptist Standard, Wisdom,* and *Ladies Home Journal*). They belonged to several mail-order book clubs, and displayed their large collection of books on floor-to-ceiling shelves in our living room. They hired a carpenter to build bookshelves in my upstairs bedroom and Mother filled them with books, hoping I would read them.

I should have been an avid reader but wasn't. I was a restless outdoors boy and a slow reader. I am still a slow reader. I wonder if I might have been dyslexic at a time when nobody had ever heard of it. I wonder about that because over the years, I have gotten a great deal of mail and feedback from people who have had some experience with dyslexia. They all made the same point, that kids with dyslexia have found the Hank books easy and pleasant to read.

Today, I meet students who are reading my books in the first and second grade. I don't remember reading much of anything until fourth grade, although Mother often read aloud to me when I was young, usually Bible stories or nature articles from *Reader's Digest*.

I started many books, sensing that it was something I ought to do, but usually jumped ship after a chapter or two. I did finish several of the Sugar Creek Gang adventures by Paul Hutchens, and enjoyed them, but beyond that and the novels of Mark Twain, I had no interest in fiction.

My reading tended to be driven by impulse and curiosity. On stormy days, I would drift over to the library wall in the living room and choose a magazine with pictures, sit down on the sofa, and turn pages until I found a subject that caught my interest. *Life* and *National Geographic* were my favorite magazines.

I also had a warm relationship with our set of World Book encyclopedias. I would choose a volume at random and spend hours turning pages, looking at the illustrations, and reading the sections that interested me.

Even today, my reading tends to follow my curiosity, and the pile of books beside my bed might include Winston Churchill's *History of the English-Speaking People*, a biography of C.S. Lewis, the memoir of a New Mexico rancher, books on ancient Egypt, modern science, Iran, mythology, and Texas Panhandle archeology. My reading follows my curiosity. The only fiction would be Hank books. I love those books and when I can't find anything else that stirs my interest, I read Hank...and laugh out loud.

Were you a good student in school?

I began my career as a student in the Perryton school system in 1950 and graduated from high school in 1962. I performed well and made good grades until the fifth grade, and at that point I began losing interest in schoolwork. As a scholar, I probably bottomed out in my sophomore or junior year in high school, when I came close to failing algebra, plane geometry, and chemistry.

Teachers don't want to hear this, but I wasn't a very good student. There was no mystery about it. I just didn't care about grades, and, oddly, I don't recall that my parents did either. I studied the bare minimum and tried to stay off the failing list.

The football coaches kept a close eye on our grades and delivered swats to the athletes whose names appeared on the failing list. In the ninth grade, I collected a number of swats and did it with pride. I even aspired to setting the school record for Most Swats in a Single Week.

That changed when Coach Ogden delivered three bombshells that almost melted my shorts. He found an effective way of saying, "Maybe you shouldn't flunk algebra." They say that when you're trying to teach a donkey, sometimes you have to start with a two-by-four.

The swats I received had nothing to do with cruelty. They were part of a game that I enjoyed until it became too painful.

In my senior year I decided to become a better student, and did the first earnest studying of my life—not enough to make me an honor student, but enough to get me accepted into college the following September.

When did you start writing?

It might sound odd, but those of us who lived in little towns in West Texas during the Fifties didn't know that becoming an author was something we could aspire to. I guess we thought that authors lived somewhere else (New York, Boston, or London), and most of them were dead.

The people in my family wrote good letters and spoke grammatical English. In fact, they were rather militant about it. Speaking careless English in our home was not tolerated. But no one in my family or town had ever written a story or novel, so we never thought that a career in writing was a possibility.

Through elementary, junior high, and most of high school, I never wrote a story or a poem, either in school or on my own. I did, however, receive serious drilling in grammar and sentence-structure, and in the eighth grade, I was introduced to sentence diagramming.

Mrs. Dunkle was our teacher, a tiny woman who wore heavy lipstick and whose dark features reminded me of Minnie Mouse. Her voice had a bit of a rasp due to her consumption of cigarettes. In spite of her size, she was not the least bit intimidated by eighth-grade boys who towered over her, played football, and thought we were tough.

In toughness, we were pretenders. She was the real deal. She had a sharp tongue that could slice up a cocksure eighth grade boy in seconds, and she did it without remorse. I know, because I tested her on several occasions. I had a special gift for luring a teacher off the subject, but it never worked on Mrs. Dunkle. She had her lesson plan, she stuck to it, and she didn't care that we considered her the meanest teacher in the entire school system.

Mrs. Dunkle was a firm believer in the importance of sentence diagramming: subject, verb, object, and modifiers. For nine months, we studied our national language as a contractor would analyze the electrical and plumbing diagrams on a blueprint. I didn't know it at the time, but it was excellent preparation for my future profession as a writer, and probably better than any kind of creative writing I might have done.

John R. Erickson in his senior year in high school.

Even today, I diagram sentences in my head, and if I were teaching a course in writing, I would begin with sentence diagramming. Thank you, Mrs. Dunkle.

It was in my senior year that I did my first creative writing and began to suspect that I might have a talent. That knowledge came my way through another English teacher, Annie Love, a dear lady who had taken on the burden of teaching Chaucer and Shakespeare to donkeys like me, and to some who were even worse than me.

Somehow, she loved us and wanted to share her deep affection for English prose and poetry. She read Chaucer aloud with the skill of an actress, actually smacking her lips as the delicious words rolled off her tongue.

When this failed to penetrate our armor-plated skulls, she called on another talent, a voice that could be as shrill as a train horn. Once provoked, she turned it on and let us have it. I'm sure that Mr. Zoller, the principal, heard complaints about Mrs. Love screeching at her kids, but I doubt that he said much about it. He knew what he had in Annie Love—an extraordinarily gifted teacher who was adored by her students—and he left her alone.

When Mrs. Love gave us the assignment of writing an original poem, I heard loud groans from other members of the football team, Johnny Leicht in particular. Johnny was a farm kid, a close friend, and always an A student. He had no trouble solving algebra equations or calculating the right answers on a chemistry exam, but the prospect of writing a poem plunged him into despair. With me, it was just the opposite. Chemistry and algebra baffled me, but somehow I knew I could write a poem.

Mrs. Love gushed over it. "Oh, this is so beautiful! Will you write me another one?" For the rest of the semester, I wrote poems for her, and she kept telling me they were beautiful. They weren't all that good—they were probably pretty bad—but her approval meant a great deal to me. I wouldn't have written poems for a grade or even for money, but I stayed up late many nights, listening to Bach and writing poems for Mrs. Love.

At certain points in a young author's life, it is very important that someone says, "This is beautiful!" She was a dear, dear lady, and years later, I dedicated one of the Hank books to her.

Were you in band or choir?

It was my good fortune to grow up in a home and community that had great respect for music. Some of my earliest memories show me listening to 78 rpm records of Prokofiev's "Peter and the Wolf," and hearing my father play classical pieces on the piano. He also served as the organist at our church. My family sang hymns in church and carols at Christmas.

John's father, Joseph Erickson, at his Yamaha grand piano. Photo by Bill Ellzey.

I began singing in church choirs when I was about four and sang in school choirs beginning in the sixth grade.

In small Texas towns, the school's music program was often a stepchild to athletics. Every school board wanted a winning football team, and some didn't care if the band and choir were an embarrassment. Perryton proved an exception to that rule, and it started at the top with Superintendent Gilbert Mize. It was Mr. Mize who hired B.D. Walker to lead the band program, and I began playing under his baton in the fifth grade. I started on the clarinet and switched to bassoon in high school.

Mr. Walker seemed a bit out of place in our conservative church-going community. He didn't spend much time in church, voted the Democrat ticket, and could be tactless in dealing with parents and lazy students. He smoked cigarettes in his office between classes and sometimes showed up in public with beer on his breath, but he knew music and produced sweepstakes-quality bands. Mr. Mize overlooked his eccentricities and backed him up.

Mr. Mize also brought Cloys Webb to our community. In high school, I sang baritone in his *a cappella* choir, and it ranks as one of the high points of my school career. We were an excellent choir because Mr. Webb insisted that we rise above our natural level of being awkward, noisy, empty-headed teenagers, living in a tiny wind-blown farm town during the age of Elvis Presley and Hank Williams.

I was awed by the power he brought to our concert performances, as he led us to heights of beauty we didn't even know existed. Under his direction, we sang some of the most sublime compositions ever to flow from the mind of a mortal being. After receiving the four-note starting pitch from the accompanist, we followed him back into sixteenth century cathedrals, singing, by memory and in Latin, compositions by Gabrieli, Schutz, Monteverdi, and Palestrina.

My love of sacred choral music began in that high school choir and has endured through a lifetime.

I was a careless student, but might have been guided by some primitive instinct that led me into activities that, years later, became important in my career as an author and performer: choir, band and stage band, speech events, and lead roles in school plays. I wrote poems for Mrs. Love, and acquired some proficiency in playing the banjo when I should have been studying chemistry.

Twenty years later, when I began recording audio book versions of the Hank the Cowdog stories and doing public performances, I put those skills to good use—skills that, in high school, were considered extra-curricular activities and didn't show up on my report cards.

When did you start playing the banjo?

My parents hoped that I would learn to play the piano, following the example of my father, who was a classically-trained pianist and church organist. I started taking piano lessons in fourth grade but never acquired a passion for it. I had natural talent and loved music, but was restless, squirmy, and lazy about practicing scales and arpeggios. I didn't want to practice. I wanted to *play*.

Mrs. Urban, my piano teacher, didn't understand such thinking. She was a disciplined musician and was raising two perfect children, Diane and Steve, who were straight-A students, and probably raced to the piano every morning to practice without being told.

During the piano lessons, my eyes tended to drift to the window and I wished that I were out in the country, working cattle with Gordon Wright and his son Bob. This must have been an early manifestation of the ranching genes that had come from my mother's side of the family, and later led me into a career as a ranch cowboy.

My sixth grade piano recital turned out to be an embarrassment for my family. I had not practiced the recital pieces and my father must have recognized that he was wasting his money on piano lessons. He gave me permission to quit—"Go on, be a cowboy, ruin your life!"—and warned that someday I would regret it. Joe Erickson was right about most things, but he was wrong about that.

My desire to *play* music, rather than practice, made me a poor student on the piano, but served me well when I took up the banjo, an instrument I discovered through my brother's record albums of Pete Seeger and The Weavers.

There was a rough honesty about Seeger's music that appealed to me. He was never a show-off kind of banjo player, the type that dazzled audiences with virtuoso three-finger picking. Seeger used his instrument to accompany the singing of The Weavers (Ronnie Gilbert, Fred Hillerman, Lee Hays, and Seeger's high tenor), and to compliment the storytelling of their songs. Seeger didn't have the greatest voice or the fastest fingers, but he was able to establish an amazing rapport with his audience.

Once I'd heard Pete Seeger, I wanted to play the banjo. In the summer of 1959 I was walking down a street in Oklahoma City with some friends. We passed a pawn shop and I saw a Kay five-string banjo sitting in the window.

I had been working all summer as a farm and ranch hand, and had a wad of cash in my pocket. I dived into the store and walked out with the banjo and a chord book. Minutes after pulling the banjo out of its cheap cardboard case, I had learned three chords and was playing Weavers songs—playing, not practicing.

Nine months later, when our high school choir made a performing tour of little towns in West Texas, I sat in the back of the bus, playing my banjo and leading other students in singing the songs of the Weavers and the Kingston Trio, the latter being a group of college boys who borrowed heavily from the Weavers and made a lot more money than the Weavers ever did.

I found Pete Seeger's approach to music fresh and original, and learned a lot about music and banjo technique from him. Years later, after I was married, I bought a book by Earl Scruggs and spent long winter evenings learning the technique he had developed, which is referred to as "three-finger picking" or "Scruggs-style picking." I found Scruggs-style picking hard to learn. It consists of a basic eight-note "roll" done with the thumb, index finger, and middle finger, and it's the style used by bluegrass banjo players.

I use Scruggs-style picking in the songs I write for the Hank audios, but very few of my songs

Photo: JRE performing in Corpus Christi in a shirt Kris bought. 'No genuine cowboy would buy such a gaudy shirt, but it sure looked good on stage.'

could be described as bluegrass music. I'm not sure they fall into any genre or style, but I know they have been shaped by the folk tradition and church music. They're just the songs that come to my mind, and I "compose" them on the banjo, using three-finger picking. I don't write them down in musical notation.

I was self-taught and am nowhere close to being an accomplished musician on the banjo, but I'm as good as I need to be and don't know what I would do if I were better.

JRE and the Stelling Staghorn banjo he lost in the wildfire of 2017.

Did you play sports in school?

In our neighborhood on Amherst Street, the boys played the sport of the season: football, basketball, baseball, volleyball, and track. Later, I played baseball and basketball on church teams, and stayed in the school's basketball program through junior high. But I wasn't good at basketball or baseball, and whatever athletic skills I possessed went into football.

In small West Texas towns, boys were not required to play football, but socially speaking, it was considered a smart move. Football was a big deal in Perryton, more prestigious than basketball, track, band, choir, drama, rodeo, or the National Honor Society.

Football games brought the entire community together, uniting students and teachers, children and parents, labor and management, Protestant and Catholic, Republican and Democrat. For three hours on Friday night, we were all Perryton Rangers.

As a boy of seven or eight, I began listening to the Ranger games on the radio. Sprawled on the floor, I followed every play and often kept a school yearbook in front of me, open to the football section that showed photographs of our star players: Don Cooper, Jimmy Todd, and Hobart Buxton (they went on to play for TCU),

JRE and cousin Mike Harter playing church league baseball in 1954.

Gene Devers, Edward Cummings, Shorty Dear, Dempsey Gyger, and others whose names were known to every boy in town.

On Saturday mornings, we played our own football games on vacant lots and argued over the right to "be" Jimmy Todd or Don Cooper.

I entered the school's football program in fifth grade, and continued all the way through my senior year in high school. What began as fun in the early grades took a serious turn in the eighth grade, when we began traveling out of town in "Old Yeller," the school's activity bus, to play teams in Pampa, Borger,

Spearman, and Canadian, Texas; Guymon, Oklahoma, and Liberal, Kansas.

Football practice acquired the rigor of boot camp. We learned to hit hard, endure pain and dehydration, and overcome humiliation and defeat.

Football in the eighth and ninth grades must have been great fun for the boys who had been blessed with early maturity. With bulging muscles and the coordination of a grown man, they harvested girls and glory, while the rest of us remained short, skinny, slow, and clumsy, and served as blocking fodder for the first team.

I didn't get my growth until the end of my freshman year, so my memories of football in the eighth and ninth grade include long, humbling practice sessions and games observed from the bench.

In the tenth grade, that began to change. I was now big enough and fast enough to make the starting lineup on Coach Beck's junior varsity, and to inflict pain upon other players. In the eleventh grade, I moved up to the varsity and played backup to our all-regional center, John D. Smith.

When two-a-day workouts started in

August of my senior year, I had to fight hard for the starting position against Danny Tarbox, a junior whose stocky build made him, on paper, a better candidate than I was for an offensive lineman.

But I was determined not to spend my senior season on the bench, and had acquired enough speed and size to win the starting position. Once there, I guarded my first-string status as a snarling dog protects a bone, and never passed up an opportunity to shatter sophomore linemen when we scrimmaged the junior varsity.

The Rangers had a successful season that year, finishing second in our district behind Quanah, and I think the coaches were surprised that I became a pretty good player. I had the wrong shape for a center (six-feet tall and 155 pounds), but I devised ways of accomplishing my mission to keep the middle guard or middle linebacker from making tackles.

The middle guards always out-weighed me, so I had to learn how to fire off the ball and deliver a stinging blow. Now and then, I conspired with the left and right guards and we invented cross-blocking patterns. I would feint a straight-ahead block, then go right or left, while Jackie Simmons or Byron Simpson blindsided the middle guard. It served to keep the toughies off balance and guessing.

When the opposing team used a six-man defensive line, I had to deal with fleet-footed middle linebackers, such as Joe Casas of Dumas. On outside plays, I pulled out and led the blocking. There was nothing in our playbook that called for the center to pull, but I did it anyway, and it worked well.

"I had the wrong shape for a center (six-feet tall and 155 pounds), but I devised ways of accomplishing my mission to keep the middle guard or middle linebacker from making tackles."

I led the running back outside the end. When the linebacker appeared behind the defensive end, I flew out of the crowd of red jerseys and took out his legs with a roll-block, which was legal at that time. We called it a "side body block."

When we played Childress, their middle guard, Jimmy Hamm, was the biggest man on the team, in fact, the biggest middle guard in the district, six-foot seven and 220 pounds. In those days, that was huge. He came into the game with a stack of press clippings, and he and his coaches took it for granted that he would give me a whipping and control the middle of the line.

That's what he told me every time I trotted out of the huddle and took my stance over the ball, that he planned to pound the everlasting snot out of me, then eat our quarterback for a snack. He talked trash.

I never talked to my opponents, only schemed. When our quarterback went back to throw a pass, Jimmy leaped high in the air to block it, all six-feet seven inches of him, and I drove my shoulder pads into his ankles.

Days later, when we watched the game film, our coaches ran that scene over and over. They loved it. Jimmy did a flip in the air and came down on his head, at which point he went into a rage and started kicking me. The referee saw it, threw a flag, and tossed him out of the game. Still fuming, and flashing dangerous glares at me, he slouched off to the sideline and watched the Childress Bobcats go down in defeat.

When did you start working on ranches?

It sometimes happens that people are changed by stories, just as trees in the Panhandle are shaped by the prevailing wind. I grew up listening to my mother's stories about Great-grandfather Joe Sherman, Grampy Buck Curry, and my great-uncles who ranched near Seminole, Texas, and Roswell, New Mexico. At an early age, working outside with soil, grass, and animals was something I wanted to do.

John R. Erickson and Nathan Ellzey working on a windmill, LZ ranch 1980. Photo by Kris Erickson.

By the time I reached junior high school, I was doing farm and ranch work for our neighbor on Amherst Street, Gordon Wright. He was a splendid man—kind, patient, warm, funny, honest, and generous, as fine a human being as ever walked the earth. He had a farm seven miles south of town, and ran a small herd of cows during the drought of the Fifties.

His son Bob and I were in the same grade in school, belonged to the same Sunday school class, lived on the same block, and became best friends, almost inseparable. Any time Bob and his dad invited me to go to the farm, I went.

Under Mr. Wright's supervision, I learned to drive a pickup and tractor, shock feed, fork silage into the back of a pickup, hunt jackrabbits, ride a horse, and work cattle. I don't recall that he ever paid me,

Proud to be a cowboy on the LZ ranch, 1980. Photo by Kris Erickson.

but I couldn't have cared less. He took the time to *teach* me and that was the best gift he could have given. And he didn't charge me for the equipment I damaged in the process of learning.

My father was an expert at finding employment for his children, and the summer after my freshman year in high school, he found me a steady job working for Henry Hale. Henry's father-in-law, Oscar Flowers, owned four sections of good farmland west of town, and a five thousand acre ranch 25 miles northwest of Perryton.

Henry and I worked hard. We hauled truckloads of alfalfa hay out of Kansas, hauled cedar posts from Mineral Wells, built fence, cleaned out stock tanks, repaired windmills, and branded calves in the spring, wrestling them down by hand.

After wheat harvest, I spent all my time on the farm, plowing wheat stubble on a John Deere tractor. I didn't enjoy the farming as much as the ranch work, but it paid better—ten dollars a day instead of eight for ranching. During plowing season, I worked twelve to fifteen hours a day. I didn't mind the long hours, the dust, the heat, or the constant noise of the tractors, which were called "Popping Johnnies" for a reason: they were loud. I wore paper wads in my ears.

I took pride in my work and wouldn't have felt the same about an inside job in town. For me, farm and ranch work had meaning. I worked for Henry throughout my high school years, and later, when I came home from college. Anytime I was back in town, I called him, and he always had plenty of work.

Part Two
Writing

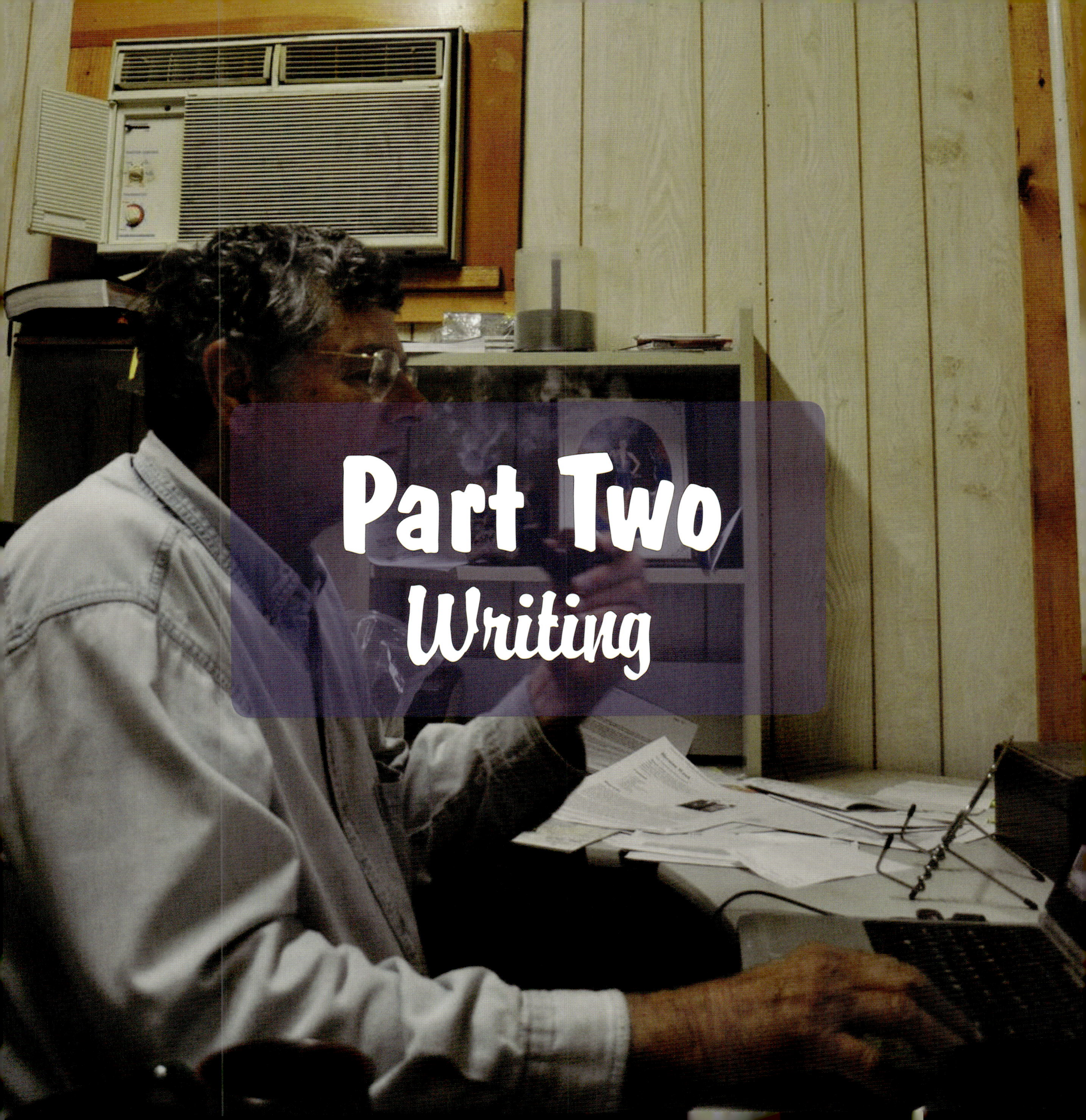

- PART TWO -

Did your parents encourage you to write?

I don't think it ever occurred to my parents, or anyone else in our community, that a kid from Perryton could be a writer. We just didn't consider it a possibility.

Even so, my mother was a good storyteller and my most important teacher. She told me stories about her kinfolks in West Texas—courageous pioneer women, ranchers, and cowboys—and flavored her stories with a gentle, earthy sense of humor.

She also read Bible stories aloud to me in the afternoons and gave me my first set of heroes. She instilled in me a sense of vocation, the idea that there was more to life than me and that I should protect my talent and use it to serve others. She must have sensed that I had a talent for doing something, although neither of us would have guessed that it would be writing.

It took me two-thirds of a lifetime to comprehend the impact she had on

Buck and Mabel Curry with Anna Beth, a dark-eyed beauty, circa 1913.

Anna Beth Curry Erickson.

me. Years later, when I was getting hundreds of rejection slips from publishers, what kept me going was nothing I had learned in a college classroom, but rather two simple sentences spoken by my mother: "God has given you a talent. You must guard it and use it wisely."

Who but a mother would say that? And who would believe anyone BUT a mother who said it?

What inspired you to become a writer?

This is one of the questions I am most-often asked, and it is usually posed in this way, in terms of "inspiration." It tells me that young readers think of writing as something one does after a ta-dah moment.

That is the way I approached writing in high school and college. At the end of a day of classroom work, if I was stirred by some emotion that needed to be expressed in a poem or essay, I stayed up late and whipped it out. When the inspiration had run its course, I might not write again for two or three weeks.

That pattern changed in 1967 when Kris and I took our wedding vows at North Park

Presbyterian Church in Dallas. All of a sudden, I was no longer a carefree bachelor who could sleep in a dumpster, stay out all night, howl at the moon, and dash off a poem once or twice a month. I had joined my life to a woman who had high standards and who expected me to do something with my life.

I had begun to suspect that being an author might be more than a passing fancy, and that it might be something I should actually try to do. It was time to get serious about it. At that point, I stopped writing at night when an inspiration seized me, and began writing every morning—*every morning*, whether I felt inspired or not. In other words, I introduced myself to the kind of discipline that is present in people who succeed in any field of endeavor, be it writing, sports, welding, playing the fiddle, or running a restaurant.

Poet Baxter Black has summed it up in one thrifty sentence: "The world is run by the people who show up." If you don't practice your fiddle, you will always be an amateur. If you don't get out of bed and start slicing vegetables, your restaurant will fail. If you don't impose discipline on your writing talent, you will spend your life talking about all the novels you're going to write, and you'll never get around to writing them.

Professional writers have professional habits. Discipline gets me out of bed and into my office, and keeps me going until inspiration shows up.

Photos - Lower left: Kristine Dykema in high school, wow! Upper right: JRE in high school. Center: John and Kris at Grandmother Curry's house in Seminole, 1972. Lower right: John and Kris at their 50th Anniversary Party.

Why did you decide to write about a dog?

I wish I could say that I planned Hank's appearance in the literary world and predicted that he would become a star, but that would be totally incorrect. Hank more or less fell into my lap after I had been writing every day for fourteen years, and I didn't recognize that there was magic in the stories until people in Perryton told me.

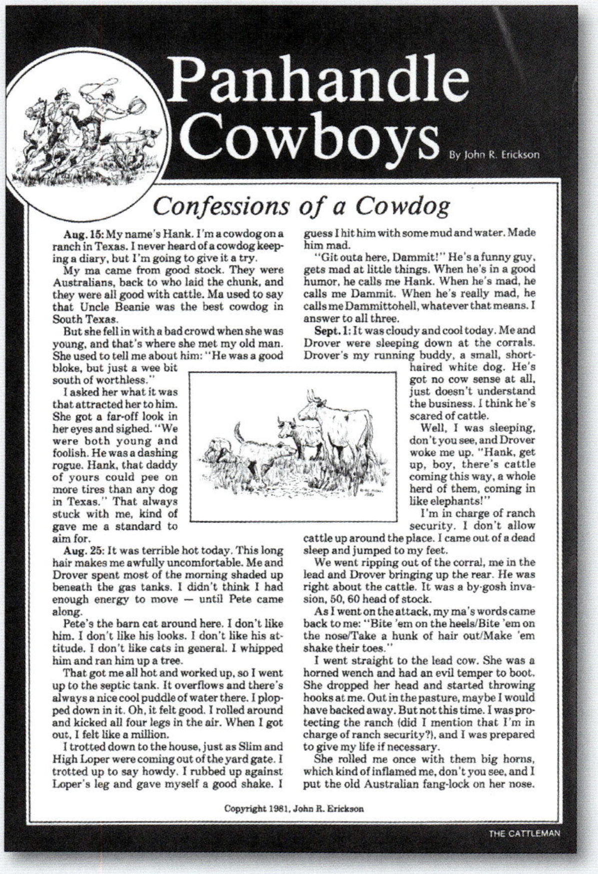

Panhandle Cowboys

By John R. Erickson

Confessions of a Cowdog

Aug. 15: My name's Hank. I'm a cowdog on a ranch in Texas. I never heard of a cowdog keeping a diary, but I'm going to give it a try.

My ma came from good stock. They were Australians, back to who laid the chunk, and they were all good with cattle. Ma used to say that Uncle Beanie was the best cowdog in South Texas.

But she fell in with a bad crowd when she was young, and that's where she met my old man. She used to tell me about him: "He was a good bloke, but just a wee bit south of worthless."

I asked her what it was that attracted her to him. She got a far-off look in her eyes and sighed. "We were both young and foolish. He was a dashing rogue. Hank, that daddy of yours could pee on more tires than any dog in Texas." That always stuck with me, kind of gave me a standard to aim for.

Aug. 25: It was terrible hot today. This long hair makes me awfully uncomfortable. Me and Drover spent most of the morning shaded up beneath the gas tanks. I didn't think I had enough energy to move — until Pete came along.

Pete's the barn cat around here. I don't like him. I don't like his looks. I don't like his attitude. I don't like cats in general. I whipped him and ran him up a tree.

That got me all hot and worked up, so I went up to the septic tank. It overflows and there's always a nice cool puddle of water there. I plopped down in it. Oh, it felt good. I rolled around and kicked all four legs in the air. When I got out, I felt like a million.

I trotted down to the house, just as Slim and High Loper were coming out of the yard gate. I trotted up to say howdy. I rubbed up against Loper's leg and gave myself a good shake. I guess I hit him with some mud and water. Made him mad.

"Git outa here, Dammit!" He's a funny guy, gets mad at little things. When he's in a good humor, he calls me Hank. When he's mad, he calls me Dammit. When he's really mad, he calls me Dammittohell, whatever that means. I answer to all three.

Sept. 1: It was cloudy and cool today. Me and Drover were sleeping down at the corrals. Drover's my running buddy, a small, short-haired white dog. He's got no cow sense at all, just doesn't understand the business. I think he's scared of cattle.

Well, I was sleeping, don't you see, and Drover woke me up. "Hank, get up, boy, there's cattle coming this way, a whole herd of them, coming in like elephants!"

I'm in charge of ranch security. I don't allow cattle up around the place. I came out of a dead sleep and jumped to my feet.

We went ripping out of the corral, me in the lead and Drover bringing up the rear. He was right about the cattle. It was a by-gosh invasion, 50, 60 head of stock.

As I went on the attack, my ma's words came back to me: "Bite 'em on the heels/Bite 'em on the nose/Take a hunk of hair out/Make 'em shake their toes."

I went straight to the lead cow. She was a horned wench and had an evil temper to boot. She dropped her head and started throwing hooks at me. Out in the pasture, maybe I would have backed away. But not this time. I was protecting the ranch (did I mention that I'm in charge of ranch security?), and I was prepared to give my life if necessary.

She rolled me once with them big horns, which kind of inflamed me, don't you see, and I put the old Australian fang-lock on her nose.

Copyright 1981, John R. Erickson

THE CATTLEMAN

The very first Hank story was a short piece that appeared in *The Cattleman* magazine, and it crossed the line between a nonfiction article and a fictional short story, in effect creating a new literary form. This occurred in such a quiet manner that even the editor didn't notice, or didn't care. That is surprising because magazine editors have strict rules about what they will and won't publish. *The Cattleman* published *no fiction*, and made that very clear in their guidelines for writers.

The Cattleman audience (cattle ranchers, predominately male) didn't read fiction, except maybe the novels of Louis L'Amour and Elmer Kelton. They didn't trust fiction and considered "fiction" another word for a lie or distortion of the truth. If you had conducted a poll of *Cattleman* subscribers and asked if they read short stories, they would have said no, absolutely not. Short stories were something for English professors and literary types Back East, the same crowd that was drawn to jazz and abstract art.

That first Hank short story *was* a work of fiction, but it blurred the hard line between imagination and fact. It operated in an environment of hard fact and observation (I knew the details of ranch life to the bone), but the entire story was narrated by a dog, which made it pure fiction. It slipped past the editor, ran in the magazine, and those old ranchers never uttered a peep.

The story allowed sunlight and humor to brighten a work of fiction, and it was handcrafted for the people in my own region and hometown.

Before Hank came along, I had spent years trying to tell stories in voices that were grammatical, educated, sophisticated, and "literary," but those attempts didn't work well. I wrote the first Hank story in a voice that fitted me like an old pair of boots. I was entirely at ease, telling a story in the voice of a ranch dog who had delusions of grandeur and wasn't very smart.

The structure of a Hank story resembles the architecture of a song. It begins with an opening statement (a G chord), builds tension (a C chord), builds more tension (a D chord), and resolves back to G. I don't like dissonant music or dissonant literature, and my stories always resolve into happy endings.

I don't think it takes a massive amount of talent or intelligence to find discord, stupidity, chaos, and evil in human events. They are easy to find. It's harder to make the chords resolve, and I think most people have a natural craving for resolution. Some literary people consider happy endings unnatural, dishonest, and silly, and sometimes they can be. I take that

Original illustration by Gerald L. Holmes from "Confessions of a Cowdog: Part Two" © 1981

risk. My stories resolve, and I don't think they're silly or dishonest.

A Hank book gives me a literary vehicle that expresses structure and meaning. In other words, it isn't just another literary howl about absurd creatures inhabiting an absurd universe. Hank is a fool and a sinner, but he's not absurd. The world he inhabits as Head of Ranch Security throbs with meaning, but with an odd twist. The events he describes are not the same ones we perceive as outside observers. Between those two poles of perception, humor leaps like an arc of electricity.

> "The world he inhabits as Head of Ranch Security throbs with meaning, but with an odd twist. The events he describes are not the same ones we perceive as outside observers. Between those two poles of perception, humor leaps like an arc of electricity."

There is a timeless quality in the Hank stories that offers some immunity to the convulsions of American popular culture: ideology, fashion, sociology, and political dogma. The stories have even overcome the taint of "regionalism," a term I often heard during my apprentice years when editors turned down my novels. Dogs are not regional. They have shared the lives and porches of human beings for at least ten thousand years, and people in China laugh just as often and just as hard at their dogs as we do in Texas.

Because I'm a slow reader, I have tailored the stories to accommodate slow readers. The books are short. I want them to be short. I use short paragraphs and short sentences, and try to make the prose simple and clear, the kind of sentences that can be diagramed: subject/verb/object. (Mrs. Dunkle would be pleased). I limit each chapter to seven double-spaced typed pages, which I judge to be the attention span of the average rancher, cowboy, and fourth grade boy — and me.

I want a Hank story to be fast, pleasant, exciting, and funny. I want the reader to laugh out loud and fly through the story. I want that slow-reading fourth grade boy to finish in a moment of triumph and yell at the top of his voice, "Hey Mom, I read a whole book!" And then dive into another one.

One of the unanticipated results of using this template is that we receive a number of letters from parents and teachers of children who are autistic, dyslexic, or just don't enjoy reading. They will read Hank books when they can't or won't read anything else.

The literary device of describing the world through the eyes and voice of a dog has given me tremendous artistic freedom. Hank's mind wanders. He loses track of what he's talking about. He misuses language and is a fountain of malapropisms. He exaggerates and winds himself up in a web of silly lies to cover his mistakes—something that children find very funny, since they do it all the time.

Hank describes things he doesn't understand. When he is terrified by the appearance of a one-eyed robot monster, we understand that he is seeing Slim Chance in a welder's hood. When he tells about his encounter with the Silver Monster Bird, he is deadly serious, but we know that he has been barking at a low-flying airplane.

Some of the funniest passages occur when Hank and Drover are awakened in the middle of the night. Half-asleep, they carry on an incoherent conversation, babbling like lunatics—exactly the way my dogs on the porch would talk if we could hear them. I sometimes feel guilty that I have been given the opportunity to write entire pages of English prose that don't make a bit of sense. They don't make sense, but they're funny.

The Hank stories have given me a medium for writing exactly the kind of stories I want to write, and that is every author's dream. Self-publishing gave me the freedom to experiment and develop the series at my own pace—without the adult supervision of people in the literary and entertainment world. I wasn't chasing a trend ("Dinosaurs are big this year") or following the recommendations of an editorial board ("We need a Hispanic dog and an Asian cat.")

It couldn't have turned out better if I had planned it all myself.

G. L. Holmes

Did you take writing courses in college?

When I was an undergraduate at the University of Texas, I never took a class on fiction writing. I'm not sure such a course was even offered. I was in a liberal arts degree program and took a number of courses on literature, and was able to do independent study projects instead of taking classes. One semester, I wrote a one-act play under a professor in the English Department, then a three-act play under a history professor.

When I was at Harvard Divinity School in 1966-68, I took a two-semester course in the Yard on fiction writing. The teacher was Professor Theodore Morrison, who had published several novels and volumes of poetry, and his former students included John Updike and Norman Mailer, who were big-name novelists at that time.

I had not written much fiction at that point and was probably lucky to get admitted into the class. Students had to submit a writing sample, and the class was limited to fifteen students.

Professor Morrison didn't actually do much teaching. He read our stories aloud to the class, and we critiqued each others' work. It seemed an odd way to teach a professional discipline, the lame leading the blind, so to speak. I mean, we were taking the class because we didn't know much about the subject, yet we were delivering editorial opinions, as though we did.

I can't say that I learned much about fiction writing in that class, but just being part of such a group encouraged me to think of myself as a writer, and to start writing every day. That might have been reason enough for taking the class, and maybe that's all I should have expected.

I won't say that taking writing courses is a bad idea or a waste of time, but if you pursue a college degree in creative writing, you should understand that it prepares you to *teach*, not necessarily

to write. I never had any desire to teach and I've had to learn on my own by writing every day, sending manuscripts to publishers, getting rejection slips, and writing some more.

I learned to write by writing—writing every day, every day, every day, and it took me fourteen years to acquire the skill to write the first Hank book. That sounds pathetic, but if there were any miracle tonics or short cuts, I didn't find them.

Panhandle boy at Harvard. Lower right: Newlyweds on the steps of Widner Library. "Clearly, she didn't marry me for my legs."

Where do you do your writing?

I write only in my writing place, and my writing places have never been fancy. All I need is enough shelf space for my books and equipment, a simple desk, and a coffee pot. Here is a list of my writing places over the years:

1967-68 in Boston: a bedroom in our apartment.

1968-70 in Austin: an extra bedroom in a house we rented.

1970-74 in Perryton: a detached garage behind our rent house. It had no plumbing or water, and it was so cold in the winter, I sometimes had to wear a coat and type with gloves.

1974-78 on a ranch in Oklahoma: I wrote in a fairly nice one-bedroom bunkhouse. It had plumbing and a good heater.

1978-80 on another ranch in Oklahoma: I wrote in a small space in a barn. It had no plumbing and was cold in the winter. Some mornings, I had to dispose of a mouse nest in the keys of my typewriter.

1980-86 in Perryton: I wrote in a garage apartment behind our house, and this was where I wrote the first Hank book. In 1982, it served as the first office/warehouse for my publishing company, Maverick Books.

1986-93 in Perryton: When we moved to a nicer house, I converted a tool shed into an office. It was small, had a cement floor and no plumbing, and was cold in the winter.

1993-2008 on our ranch in Roberts County: I wrote in an old bunkhouse about a mile from our home. I spent a lot of hours writing in this shack, and it was pretty rustic. Water came from a windmill nearby and it froze every winter. The house had mice, pack rats, and bats. One time I caught a bull snake in a mouse trap. Raccoons and skunks lived under the house, and one morning my faithful dog Sophie got into a fight with a skunk. It changed the smell of my office for weeks. That bunkhouse gave me a lot of ideas for Slim Chance's bachelor shack.

In 2008, our son Scot found a 10 x 30 foot structure that had been used as a temporary office at a construction site in Amarillo. He hired a truck and a crane and moved it to a spot on the ranch west of our house. He and a crew hooked it up to water and electricity, and our son-in-law, Randy Wilson, added a screened-in porch on the south. It was big enough to hold my books, desk, and a filing cabinet. It had a small wood burning stove that I used when the electricity went out in the winter, and I sometimes wrote on the screened porch in the summer months. There, I could watch the wild turkeys marching off to work and the buzzards leaving their roosting tree up the canyon.

It was as good an office as I could have wanted, and it was there that I wrote most of this book, as well as a number of Hank books. On March 6, 2017, that office was destroyed in a wildfire. (See Section Five)

JRE in his writing office at the ranch, 2015. He lost the office and his library in the wildfire of 2017. Photo courtesy of Lumindeo.

Do you follow a certain routine in your writing?

Writing isn't glamorous work, and I often think of myself as a mule pulling a plow around a field. I have developed the routine of rising early, usually around 5:30, and seldom remain in my office after 10:00 a.m. When I was working as a cowboy in the Seventies, there were days when I had to start at 4:30 in order to get a couple of hours of writing time.

If I have already started a writing project, I begin the morning's work by reading over the pages I wrote the day before, making revisions and corrections, then start writing new material. If I don't have a project in mind…that's when writing gets tough. I have already committed to stay in my office for at least four hours and don't allow myself to cheat. I have to sit there and do something: stare at the walls or write.

Some days I have no ideas or inspiration. I read and revise Hank books that are written but not published, write letters, or write in my journal. Maybe I'll work on an article. Over the years, I have published seven or eight hundred articles (I lost count long ago). They're not as satisfying as Hank books, but I enjoy doing them and they bring some relief from the boredom of sitting there.

Boredom is painful, but I'm a firm believer that it can be used to spur us into productive behavior. That might sound odd, since we live in a time when boredom is viewed as an enemy. Entire industries have been built to spare us from even a moment of boredom. We have the radio, television, iTunes, YouTube, video games, social media, and phone texting to rescue us from the dull ache of boredom, but at the end of a day or week, what have they gotten us? Not much that we can be proud of.

At ten o'clock I leave my office and spend the rest of the day doing other things. We live on a cattle ranch and I have found that ranch work is a good compliment to the intensity of writing. The ranch work is physical. It draws me outside of my head and into my body, into the world. I spend most of my time with animals and those experiences provide me with material for my writing.

It's important that I strike a balance between the mental and physical. If I spent too much time doing mental work, I would lose contact with the physical world around me: trees, sunsets, weather, people, dogs, the seasons, and honest sweat. And, eventually, that weakness would show up in my writing.

Where do you get the ideas for your stories?

When I was in college and starting to think about becoming an author, it didn't occur to me that I could write about the place where I had grown up. As far as I knew, authors came from big cities and they wrote about "important" places, which didn't include any of the little towns in the Texas Panhandle.

After completing my first year of college, I took a summer job working in a church in New York, and I loved the city. Later, I spent two years living in the Boston area while I attended Harvard Divinity School. I took it for granted that I would end up living in one of those places and writing about life in the city.

What I discovered, though, was that my heart was not in those places. I just didn't belong there, and my writing lacked something, truth or passion or whatever it is that brings a sparkle to a piece of writing.

In 1968, Kris and I moved back to Texas, and in 1974 I did something I never would have predicted: I took a job managing a 5,000 acre ranch in Beaver County, Oklahoma, about 60 miles north of Perryton. In 1978 we moved

JRE's office until 2017. Photo courtesy of Lumindeo.

to another ranch in Beaver County, and in 1979 I took a job working for the LZ ranch, south of Perryton.

During this period, I was writing 3-4 hours every morning, then going out and working as a cowboy—and I wasn't playing cowboy; it was the real deal. I got no passes for being a writer. The combination of physical work and the mental/emotional demands of writing suited me well, and I began incorporating my cowboy experiences into my writing. At some point, after years of trial and error, I began to realize that this was what I was supposed to be writing about.

The moment of clarity came in 1982-83, when I wrote and self-published the first Hank the Cowdog book. I was shocked by the response of my readers. They loved it and began the chorus, "Keep writing Hank books!"

As a young man, I had thought (immodestly) that I could write about anything I chose, but it didn't turn out that way. To some extent, the subject chooses the writer, not the other way around, because honest writing comes from the heart. You can choose your clothes, but not your skin or your heart. I sometimes lament that it took me fifteen years to learn this (what a bonehead!), but I have a history of being a slow learner, and I can't complain about the way things have turned out.

For whatever reason, I can't seem to write about anything but ranch life, ranch work, and the people and animals

JRE with Arabian sisters, Nocona and Windsong. Photo by Nathan Dahlstrom.

who are involved in this way of life, and that has become the source abyss for all my stories. If I had stopped doing ranch work in 1983, when we brought out the first Hank book, I could not have kept the series going, certainly not to its present level of 74 books.

I would have exhausted my source of story material. To keep the stories going, I've had to maintain close contact with ranch life.

My story material comes from my experiences every day on our ranch: cattle, horses, dogs, cats, wildlife, weather, and people. It all goes into the compost heap, and when it's time for me to write another Hank book, somehow it comes together in the shape of a short novel, narrated by a dog. I often begin a story with whatever is going on around me that day: the fragrance of spring grass, dogs snoozing in the shade on a hot summer day, a cold north wind moaning outside, a snow storm, an ice storm, or the spirit-sapping effects of a drought.

I often get story ideas during a church service, although these tend to be less specific than the ones I get on the ranch. The atmosphere inside a church is quite different from the world we experience in other places. The architecture, scripture readings, rituals, and music draw us into a deeper

Upper: Cowboy crew on the M-cross ranch. Photo Nathan Dahlstrom.
Lower: Crossing the Canadian River: JRE, Bobby Barnett, and Nathan Dahlstrom. Photo by Kris Erickson.

dimension of time, to people who lived and died at least two thousand years ago, and to ideas that have survived for three millennia. This brings a perspective to the writing process that you wouldn't get, say, in a shopping mall or at a football game.

Funerals bring an even deeper experience, especially when the death was unexpected and tragic. In a small town, we can't escape the grief that comes from the death of a child or a young mother or father, and we come together in a church service to find strength as a whole community. It reminds me that what I do as a writer is part of that community. I want to contribute something that makes it better and stronger.

The First United Methodist Church In Perryton. Photo courtesy of Lumindeo.

Do you write Hank books every day?

No. I wish I could, because writing Hank books is so much fun, it's like eating ice cream. Unfortunately, we can't eat ice cream every day.

Years ago, when I realized that Hank was a popular character and that his adventures would become an ongoing series, I had to figure out how to pace myself. How many Hank books could I write in a year?

We have discussed the balance between mind and body. This brings up another example of finding a balance, the balance between source material and productivity. See, we're not talking about "cranking out" one book after another. We're talking about writing *good* stories, books that maintain the quality my readers deserve and have come to expect.

Here, I find some parallels between writing and ranching. Ranchers think of themselves as stewards of land and animals, not just owners. A good steward cares for the resources under his management. It's his job to use them wisely and keep them strong and healthy, but it's more than just a job. It has a spiritual dimension. Good stewardship connects us to things bigger than ourselves, to our Source and purpose.

If you run too many cattle on your land, you abuse the grass. You might get by with that in good-moisture years, but eventually it will catch up with you. If you over-graze your pastures, you punish the land you're supposed to be taking care of.

Or let's suppose you have a milk cow that can produce a gallon of milk every day for your family, but you think she should produce more. You give her special feed and vitamin pills and goose up her milk production to three gallons a day. It works for a while. She produces more milk...until she drops dead from fatigue. In that case, you have not been a good steward of your resource.

I want to be a good steward of the

Hank franchise, and that means I must provide my readers with a good, exciting, funny Hank adventure every time. I have found that I can deliver two good stories per year, and I've been doing it now for thirty-six years.

That is an accomplishment I'm proud of, and I've been told that Hank is the longest-running children's series in America—written by one author. Most long-running series (The Boxcar Children, Goosebumps, and The Hardy Boys, for example) require the services of more than one author. Even though the author's name remains the same, the publisher uses "ghost writers" to keep the series going.

I have never used a ghost writer. Every word of every book was written by the guy whose name appears on the front cover. Me.

Is it possible that I could have written three good Hank books per year, instead of just two? Instinct has told me not to try it. To quote a very good wise old saying, "If it ain't broke, don't fix it."

How long does it take to write a Hank book?

The first one was the hardest to write. It took me fifteen years to find the subject material that was right for me. During that period, I was writing four hours every day and sending off manuscripts to publishing companies that sent them back with rejection slips. By the time I stumbled into Hank and wrote the first book, I was so discouraged, I didn't bother sending it off to a publisher or agent. I started Maverick Books and published it myself.

Once I had discovered Hank, the writing process became much easier. I wrote the second book in two weeks, which I still find astonishing. In terms of speed, I haven't matched that in the years since. Let's be honest: producing a good book in two weeks is a rare accomplishment.

Since then, the process of writing a Hank book has fallen into a routine that is fairly predictable. When it's time to start a new book, I begin by writing the first sentence, and I always know what it will be: "It's me again, Hank the Cowdog." Years ago, I read an article in *Writer's Digest* in which an author claimed that the hardest part of producing a new book was coming up with the first sentence, so I have taken care of that. I type out the first sentence and then all I have to do is finish the book.

I have written non-Hank books that stretched out over many months, even more than a year, but Hank books are different. I want them to be read quickly and they should be written quickly. It usually takes me four to six weeks to write one, and that means writing four hours per day, seven days a week. If I don't have the story under control in four to six weeks, it usually means that something is wrong.

Once I have finished a story, I put it away and might not go back to it for months. I have a file on my computer for books that are finished but unpublished, and there are always at least five finished books in the file. In other words, I am always five books ahead, and most new books sit for three years before they go to the printer.

I don't want to write against a deadline. I would find it stressful, but more importantly, if I were racing a deadline, I might be tempted to accept a story that was second-rate. Under my system, I'm able to let a book sit for three years, and during that time, I will go back and reread it fifteen or twenty times. On every reading, I give it a polish. I want it to be as smooth as a piece of fine furniture.

"I don't want to write against a deadline. I would find it stressful, but more importantly, if I were racing a deadline, I might be tempted to accept a story that was second-rate."

Emotional distance brings clarity to the writing process, and on six occasions, I have read a finished book and come to the conclusion that it wasn't good enough. It had spots that seemed dead or wooden, and might give a reader the impression that the author began the story thinking, "Well, it's time to crank out another one."

I try to hold Hank books to a higher standard, and "cranking" one out isn't good enough. When a book doesn't measure up, I throw it out of the lineup.

What became of those six books I threw out? I submitted them to a merciless revision and chopped out all the dead spots, which left me with about fifty percent of the original story. I shortened the chapters and turned them into serial stories that we have run in newspapers and magazines.

I have also recorded them as audio books, so even though they have never appeared in book form, they are available as "audio-only" stories.

I am satisfied with them in the shortened versions, and I would say they are good stories. They include: *The Homeless Pooch, The Dancing Cowboy, Cookie Moon, The Runaway Windmill, The Watermelon Patch Mystery*, and *The Valentine's Day Robbery.*

hours later, I had written Chapter Four, "The Boxer."

Once I had gotten the story moving again, the writing must have come without effort, because there is no mention of it in my journal until October 8, when I made an astonishingly casual entry: "I have finished *Hank the Cowdog and the Chicken House Murders*. Ready to send it to the typesetter."

By that time, Maverick Books was rolling. We had sold 1200 copies of *The Devil in Texas* in a little more than a month, had ordered a second printing, and had decided to bring out the new Hank book in the spring. Those were busy times and the Hank book received no coddling. Kris read the manuscript and suggested changes, I did the revisions, and we sent it to Tom Sheahan, our book designer and typesetter in Omaha.

Sheahan suggested that we drop "The Chicken House Murders" from the title. He thought it sounded too harsh. I didn't agree with him, but we changed it.

What books, if any, have influenced your writing?

During my years as an aspiring novelist (1967-82), I did a great deal of reading in literature: popular novels of the time, literary fiction, classics, and novels by authors from Texas and the West. I am something of a mimic, and often tried to incorporate an author's style and technique into the stories I was writing.

I was probably most influenced by the novels of Elmer Kelton and Herman Wouk. Both wrote lucid prose, told good stories, and wrote for a general audience—that is, they weren't writing for a small group of literary critics, university professors, or other writers.

I was particularly interested in Elmer's work because we shared a common cultural background. He was raised on a ranch in West Texas, attended school in the small town of Crane, graduated from the University of Texas, settled down in San Angelo, and chose to write novels about an area that many people in the publishing world considered "too regional" — West Texas.

I had great respect for Elmer, as a man and as a writer, and at one time I would have been pleased to imitate his success as an author of entertaining, well-written, well-researched western novels, but somehow that didn't work out for me. When Hank walked into my life, I stopped trying to imitate other writers and turned my full attention to my life's work, writing funny stories narrated by a dog.

By the way, Elmer Kelton bought Hank books for his grandchildren.

In the 1970s, when I was working on ranches, I discovered the novels of Herman Wouk: *Marjory Morningstar, The Caine Mutiny, The Winds of War,* and *War and Remembrance*. I set out to read everything he had written and made a serious study of his technique.

That I saw Herman Wouk as a model and teacher seems odd, because we could hardly have been more different. Wouk (like me) who didn't sit around reading books. Tom and Huck were drawn to great adventures: fishing, camping, exploring, playing hooky from school, and rafting on the Mississippi River. That was the life for me, and those books seized my imagination.

The quality in Twain's writing that impressed me most was his use of humor. *The reader was allowed to laugh!* Reading didn't have to be a drab, joyless experience, and for me at that age, it usually was. I loved the way he used regional dialects and played with language, like a dog chasing butterflies through a field of wildflowers.

"The quality in Twain's writing that impressed me most was his use of humor. The reader was allowed to laugh! Reading didn't have to be a drab, joyless experience, and for me at that age, it usually was."

I have tried to capture that playful spirit in the Hank books, and Mark Twain's fingerprints are all over them. When I get a fan letter from a fourth grade boy who says, "I hate to read, but I love your books," I smile and think of myself at that age, and of Mark Twain.

Today, I wonder if I would have ever discovered Hank the Cowdog if Mrs. Smith had not gone to the trouble of reading *Tom Sawyer* to her class. It's another example of how deeply teachers can touch the lives of their students.

Herman Wouk was also touched by Mark Twain: "Twain, with a seven-league stride of genius, went and diverted the broad river of English prose into a free-running American stream, murmuring a clear new music that a sixth-grader son of immigrant Russian Jews could hear."

Sherlock Holmes. I have never been a reader of detective fiction, but during the early 1980s, I borrowed a collection of Sherlock Holmes stories from my father's library and gave it a careful reading. Years later, Kris and I acquired the entire BBC series of Sherlock Holmes videos (about fifty of them), starring the incomparable Jeremy Brett as Holmes. We have watched them many times, and I suspect that I owe a nod of gratitude to Arthur Conan Doyle.

When I began writing the Hank books, I wasn't thinking of Sherlock Holmes or trying to imitate Conan Doyle, but there might be a genetic link between

Hank and Holmes. Both are featured in a long-running series of stories involving two main characters (Holmes-Watson, Hank-Drover), one of whom is dedicated to solving criminal cases.

Both Holmes and Hank are self-preoccupied and devoid of humor. The Hank stories are funny, but Hank himself is as humorless as a cinder block. So is Sherlock Holmes. The ultimate joke in the Hank stories is that he has no self-knowledge, isn't very smart, misses the most important clues in a case, and doesn't know what he's talking about half the time. The reader knows, but Hank doesn't, and that is funny.

I think a case could be made that, to some extent, Hank is a parody of Sherlock Holmes—the great British detective with floppy ears and a big nose. It wasn't something I set out to do on a conscious level, but there it is.

One of the highest compliments I've received on the Hank series came from a New York publishing executive, who said, "Oh no, they're not children's stories. They're great literature, like Sherlock Holmes."

Is it true that you didn't write the Hank books for kids?

Yes, and it's a little embarrassing. I'm the author of one of the most popular book series for children in America, and I know nothing about children's literature. That's not an exaggeration. I really don't.

When I wrote *The Original Adventures of Hank the Cowdog*, Kris served as my editor, and after reading the manuscript, she said, "This would make a great children's story." In a flash of anger, I growled, "It's not a children's book! I don't write children's books."

I find it interesting that Livy Clemens, Mark Twain's wife, gave the same response when she read *Tom Sawyer* in manuscript. She said it was a book for boys. In a letter to a friend, Twain fumed, "It is *not* a boy's book, at all. It will only be read by adults. It is only written for adults." Several months later, he wrote the same friend, saying that he had come to agree with Livy: it was a book for boys.

As usual, Kris's instincts were right on target. My original audience consisted mostly of adults involved in agriculture, but the circle began to widen and children started reading the books. It was a natural phenomenon that happened on its own, without any scheming or advertising.

I can only guess how it occurred. Families read the book aloud on trips or around the dinner table, or parents read the books and passed them on to their children. By the time we had brought out the third episode in

1984, I was getting calls from teachers and librarians who wondered if I would come to their schools and do a program.

When I replied that the humor was too subtle for children, the teachers informed me that students were bringing the books to school and reading them at recess on the playground. "They think they understand the humor. They're laughing."

At some point, I did the sensible thing—stopped arguing with my audience and accepted that I had become an author of children's books. It was a blessing that it happened this way, without any scheming on my part, because had I been trying to write for children, I would have written *down* to the audience, and that would have been a mistake.

Children don't catch all the jokes or understand all the puns and plays on language, but they understand more of the subtle humor than I ever dreamed possible. Years later, when they read Hank books to their own children, they will enjoy the parts they missed when they were young.

Where did you get the idea for Hank's title "Head of Ranch Security"?

In the summer of 1982, I contracted with *Equus* magazine to do a series of twelve articles on Buster Welch and the King Ranch's cutting horse program, and it required considerable time and travel. I had to make two trips to interview Buster on his ranch near Abilene, and make another trip to the King Ranch in South Texas.

I flew to Corpus Christi, rented a car, and drove to the King Ranch just outside of Kingsville. I spent the first day looking at some magnificent Quarter Horses and interviewing Joe Stiles, who was in charge of the horse program. That evening, I attended a picnic for Joe's employees and met his father, Leonard Stiles.

Leonard had worked many years as a Special Ranger for the Texas and Southwest Cattle Raisers Association, and now served as Head of Ranch Security on the King Ranch, one of the biggest ranches in Texas. He was a tall, well-built, handsome man who held himself ramrod straight and had a pair of eyes that could pierce steel.

During the picnic, while everyone else chatted and played volleyball, Leonard's eyes never rested. Any time a vehicle passed, he was watching.

I thought to myself that if I ever wrote a novel about an old-time Texas Ranger, I would use Leonard Stiles as the pattern. If all Texas Rangers didn't look like Leonard Stiles, they should. I could imagine that his stern face had been an effective tool in melting confessions out of many a cattle thief.

I never got around to writing a novel about a Texas Ranger, but I'm certain that Hank's self-anointed title of Head of Ranch Security came from the evening I spent with Leonard Stiles.

Several years later, I saw him and his wife at a Cattle Raisers convention and told them. The flint-eyed ranger actually smiled and said it made him proud, because his grandchildren were reading the books.

I have made two author appearances at the Santa Gertrudis Elementary School in Kingsville, where all the children of King Ranch employees go to school. I was pleased to tell them about this link between Hank and the ranch.

How did you meet Gerald Holmes, the illustrator?

We met in 1976 at the country home of a mutual friend, cowboy photographer Bill Ellzey. That house later became Slim Chance's bachelor shack in the Hank books. At that time, Gerald was working in a feedlot near Perryton and I was working on a ranch in Beaver County, Oklahoma. We were both as poor as sparrows in winter. Between the two of us, we would have been lucky to raise enough money to buy a cup of coffee.

Gerald grew up on a ranch near Waurika, Oklahoma, and knew ranch life to the bone. He showed me some of his pen and ink drawings and I liked them at once. He seemed to be doing with pictures the sort of thing I wanted to do with words: describing ranch life in a manner that was honest, funny, and aesthetically pleasing.

He started doing pen and ink drawings to illustrate

Gerald L. Holmes at work. With a few strokes of his pencil, he creates faces for the characters in the books. Photos courtesy of Lumindeo.

move (some would say crazy), but we felt that I was writing the kind of stories that people in our area wanted and needed, and that we could find an audience. We didn't need the approval of editors or critics. We needed customers, and we thought we could find them right where we lived.

I sold books at rodeos, county fairs, and trade shows, in saddle shops, western wear stores, small town drug stores and grocery stores. I started doing readings for groups in Perryton, then programs in schools and for groups of teachers. At every stop, I sold books and autographed every one of them.

The circle grew and people kept saying, "More Hank books!" So I wrote Hank books and we kept bringing them out. In 1985 I had five employees and the business could no longer fit into the garage apartment behind our house, so we moved to a suite of offices downtown.

Money was flying in and flying out, but I couldn't tell if I was getting rich or going broke. I hired an accounting student from Wayland Baptist University to spend the summer going through our records, and in September he said things were going in the wrong direction. When he graduated the next spring, I hired him to run the business, and Gary Rinker has been my partner ever since. He is a good, honest man and has played a vital role in the success of our Hank adventure.

In 1986, after we had brought out ten Hank books and established a name for the brand, we changed course and Gary negotiated contracts with larger, more established companies to take over the publishing and distribution of the books: Texas Monthly Press, Gulf Publishing, and the Penguin Group. They succeeded in getting the books into the distribution mainstream, wholesalers and bookstores, which is something we had not done well.

In 2010, Penguin didn't renew our contract, so we brought everything back home to Maverick Books and Perryton. That's where

The Maverick Books display at the 1983 National Finals Rodeo carried only two Hank books. Photo by Kris Erickson.

Gary and Kim Rinker, 1998.

we are today, in a warehouse on the west edge of town, so things have come full circle. When you buy a Hank book or CD on Amazon or in a bookstore, it originated in our warehouse in Perryton, boxed up by Gary or Kim Rinker.

Self-publishing wasn't my first choice, but it gave me options that I couldn't have gotten under the standard system. First, it gave me a way out of a game that seemed rigged against me. Self-publishing allowed me to get my stories in front of the public and to build an audience from scratch.

I don't think a major publisher would have touched the first Hank book. Not only was it "too regional," but it was odd, quirky, and thoroughly unconventional. I had to prove that readers would buy a book narrated by a not-very-smart dog who claimed he was Head of Ranch Security.

Second, self-publishing gave us creative control of the stories. Every word in those books was written by me (no outside ghost writers) and the stories reflect the history, folkways, and values of the community where I live. Kris and I go to church there, our kids attended school there, that's where we buy our groceries. My parents and Kris's mother are buried in the cemetery south of town.

The books have to be good enough for the people in my hometown, and that is a high standard of quality. I have great respect for them. After all, they were the original audience who said, "You need to do more with that dog."

Third, self-publishing allowed us to maintain control of all the subsidiary rights, including movie, television, and merchandising. If the Hank books had started out with a big publisher, I would have lost the right to negotiate movie and television contracts. In today's world, with the standards of popular culture in decline, that has become an important issue.

Do you know any other writers?

There was a time, early in my career, when I had a strong desire to meet other writers. I had grown up in a place where, as far as I knew, writers didn't exist, so naturally I was curious. Actually, there were a few writers in Amarillo and Canyon—Luella Grace Erdman, Olive K. Dixon, J. Evetts Haley, John McCarty, and Al Dewlen—but for some reason we didn't hear about them in school. That's a pity, because they all lived in the Panhandle and did good work.

I didn't meet a real-live author until I was twenty and a student at UT. My history professor, Paul F. Boller, Jr., had published several books and recognized that I had a talent for writing. Both semesters in his American history class, I made A's because he gave essay tests and I wrote good essays. He encouraged me to develop my writing skills and gave me good advice: "You learn to write by writing."

After college, I made an effort to meet Texas authors. In 1972, I knocked on the doors of J. Evetts Haley in Canyon and Al Dewlen in Amarillo, and had the opportunity to spend several hours with each of them. In 1973 I spent a pleasant afternoon with Bill Wittliff in Austin, years before he wrote the screenplay for "Lonesome Dove." That same year, I met John Graves, author of *Goodbye to a River*, one of the finest books written by a Texan. We remained friends until his death and I dedicated one of the Hank books to him and his wife Jane.

In 1978 I joined the Western Writers of America and attended their conventions for eight years.

The lean and hungry author of Hank the Cowdog. Photo by Kris Erickson.

That's where I met Elmer Kelton, a novelist I admired very much, and we became friends. I met Don Coldsmith, Jeanne Williams, Gary McCarthy, Jory Sherman, Don Worcester, Jim Jennings, Spike Van Cleve, and other writers. I never met Louis L'Amour but heard him speak at the WWA convention in Santa Rosa, California. He was in his eighties and a very impressive man.

In the Eighties and Nineties, I performed at cowboy poetry gatherings in Lubbock and Elko, Nevada, and became acquainted with Red Steagall, Waddy Mitchell, and Baxter Black, among the best-known of the cowboy poets. At author functions, I had brief encounters with Elmore Leonard, Bill Porterfield, Larry King, Molly Ivins, A.C. Greene, Steve Allen, Bill Wallace, Larry McMurtry, and Edwin Shrake. I wish I could have met Ben K. Green. He was an eccentric old man from Cumby who had forgotten more about cattle and horses than most of us will ever know, and a great storyteller.

At some point, I lost my desire to spend time with authors. Maybe I had learned whatever I needed to know and was pretty well established on my own course. John Graves once told me, "We writers aren't very interesting people. The best of what we are goes into our books." I also realized that it was a better use of my time to seek out readers, not other writers. I dropped out of WWA and the Texas Institute of Letters, and concentrated on doing Hank programs in schools. In those settings, I was surrounded by readers and never saw another author.

I did, however, maintain an active exchange of letters with Elmer Kelton, Baxter Black, and John Graves, and corresponded on two occasions with novelist Herman Wouk, whom I consider one of the great authors of our time, maybe the greatest. I was honored that he took the time to write me back. Unfortunately, all my letters from those author-friends were destroyed in the wildfire of 2017.

In recent years, I haven't had much contact with other writers. Baxter Black and I talk on the phone once in a while, and I have maintained a close friendship with S.J. Dahlstrom, a young author in Lubbock who writes the Wilder Good series of novels.

What is the Ranch Life Series and why did you write those books?

The Ranch Life Series is a collection of nonfiction books we have brought out in a joint effort with the National Ranching Heritage Center in Lubbock, Texas. I wrote them sometime around 2002 to explain ranch life, ranch work, livestock, and the cattle business to young readers who probably didn't know much about those subjects.

Hanging out in school libraries between performances, I had looked at books on these subjects, published by big New York firms and written by authors who also lived in New York. It was safe to assume that those writers had little or no first-hand experience with ranching and cowboy work, and had gotten all their information out of books written by someone else—by me, for example. I had written seven nonfiction books and hundreds of articles on ranch life and cowboy work, and they were all grounded on personal experience.

It irked me that kids in my part of Texas were being offered books about our ranching heritage, written by people who were never a part of it, so I decided to write my own books for kids and publish them myself through Maverick Books. I didn't have to buy a big hat and a pair of boots to prove that I knew about cowboying, because I was one. I wrote about my lifetime of experience with horses, cattle, and cowboy work, but instead of speaking in my

John Erickson voice, I used the voice of old Hank, a voice kids already knew and trusted.

I wrote three books, but Gary Rinker and I didn't know what to do with them. We got busy with other things and forgot about them. Thirteen years passed. One day in 2015, I was in Lubbock on a speaking trip and drove past a sign that said, "National Ranching Heritage Center." I had known about this fine institution for decades and had even performed there, but had never thought about talking to them about those old dust-covered Ranch Life books. The NRHC defines its purpose as "preserving and interpreting the history of ranching heritage of North America and addressing contemporary ranching issues." It seemed a good match.

I drove to the museum, just north of the Texas Tech campus, and introduced myself to Julie Hodges, who had recently taken the position of Director of Education for the NRHC. I told her about the series and was pleased by her enthusiastic response. With an air of quiet confidence, she said, "I think we can figure out what to do with those books."

Indeed she did. We brought out the first book, about ranching and livestock, in 2016 and a private donor paid for a printing of five thousand copies, enough to provide a free book to every fourth grader in the metropolitan area around Lubbock. We brought out the second book, about horses and cowboy work, in 2017, and another donor paid for five thousand copies. We brought out the third book about wildlife in 2018, and I have written a fourth book about prairie fires.

In the meantime, Julie worked with two Lubbock teachers, Michelle Sedberry and Jenna Gaona, to produce teacher workbooks that incorporate the Ranch Life Series into a school's curriculum in social studies and science. The folks at the NRHC are pleased to make this a part of their public outreach. The teachers are pleased to incorporate our local ranching and cowboy heritage into their education programs, and I am pleased that children in my region are getting solid information about subjects that are dear to my heart.

Do you have a Hank the Cowdog website?

Those of us who have been involved in the world of Hank the Cowdog for decades tend to be low-tech, shall we say. We've had to learn how to use computers and mail-order software as tools of business, and we've adapted to smartphones, but in our deepest hearts, we are people who enjoy holding a real book in our hands and have not been inclined to plunge with wild abandon into the Internet.

Several years ago, my son Mark informed me that our Maverick Books website was crude and dysfunctional, an embarrassment. He said that even though we were a small regional press, we were operating in a global marketplace where the standard of excellence was Amazon, and Amazon is very good at what they do.

By this time, we had hired Nikki Georgacakis Earley to do book design and marketing, and she agreed with the verdict of my bossy son. They checked out web designers in Austin and Dallas, and selected one to upgrade our system. Nikki didn't think of herself as high-tech, but she made a study of Internet marketing and has taken it upon herself to bring us at least partway into the twenty-first century.

She runs the Hank website, hankthecowdog.com, where viewers can find news about us, a schedule of my personal appearances, links to interviews and news events, a special section for teachers, and a blog with articles I have published. We also have an online store that offers the most complete line of Hank merchandise you can find anywhere, and that includes Amazon.

Nikki also has links to Facebook and other social media outlets. Kris and I don't use Facebook (oddly enough, neither does Nikki), but I go to the Hank FB page almost every day to see what she has posted. It might be pictures that fans have sent, photos from our ranch, or a link to something on YouTube. Two or three times

Nikki Earley, photo by Kris Erickson.

a week, she posts a Gerald Holmes drawing from one of the books, with a funny caption that fits the picture.

There is a way of going to the FB pages of people who have left comments on our site, and I enjoy doing that from time to time.

They live in all parts of the U.S., though the number of fans in the Northeast is a bit sparse. There was a time when you could count on finding several comments from people in Iran. Our books have been translated into Farsi (illegally) and we have a surprising number of fans there, which I think is nice.

But in the past several years, that has changed. I don't find Iranian names anymore. I've wondered if the government of Iran has tightened its rules about access to Western sites on the Internet. If so, that's a pity. The Persians need a good laugh as much as the rest of us.

Do you get a lot of fan mail?

I get quite a lot of mail, both as paper letters and emails to the Hank website. I get birthday cards and Christmas cards. Many of the paper letters come with drawings or photographs of dogs. I get mail from girls as well as boys, adults as well as children, and sometimes whole families. I get big envelopes from an entire class of students, with a note from the teacher.

I get requests from people who want to drive to Perryton and meet me. I'm flattered but don't know how to respond without seeming rude. I don't spend much time in town and we live forty miles in the country, in a very isolated part of the

Canadian River valley. It's not a simple matter for me to meet people unless they come to my public appearances or to our church on Sunday—and some people have done that.

I answer paper letters with a nice card that Nikki Earley designed for me, with a color drawing by Gerald Holmes. It shows Slim Chance sitting on a bale of hay, poking the keys on an old manual typewriter while Hank sleeps at his feet and Drover and Pete watch. I write a short response by hand.

After we lost our home in the wildfire of 2017, word spread and I received a huge outpouring of sympathy boxes of mail, so much that I gave up trying to read it all. Before the fire, I was pretty scrupulous about answering every letter and email, because I understood that getting a fan letter is a great compliment. I never want to take it for granted. I try to remember all those years when I was living on ranches, writing four hours every morning, sending out manuscripts to publishers, and getting rejection slips. I dreamed of the day when someone would write me a fan letter.

After the fire, I lost my cards, my office, my daily routine, and haven't quite gotten back into the pattern of answering every letter and email, and I don't feel right about it. That experience of losing everything changed a lot of things and it might take a while to get back to where we were before.

Unopened mail after the 2017 fire. Photo by Nikki Earley.

Have your books been translated into other languages?

Most publishing companies have people on the staff who are actively involved in trying to sell translation rights. They attend trade shows in places like Frankfurt, Paris, and Moscow, and make deals. Maverick Books is kind of a mom-and-pop operation, consisting of me and Kris, Gary and Kim Rinker, and Nikki Earley, and there are some things we don't do particularly well. Nobody at our shop wants to attend the Frankfurt Book Fair, and we make no effort to sell translation rights.

Even so, some foreign publishers have tracked us down and inquired about translation rights. Gary handles those calls and has negotiated contracts for translations into Chinese, Swedish, Danish, and Spanish. Years ago, he got a call from a man who had translated twenty books into Farsi, the language of Iran. He explained that Iran has no diplomatic relations with the U.S. and thus no treaty for dealing with copyrights, so his company publishes translations of English books, without contracts or permission. He regretted that we would never receive any royalties, but said the books are popular in Iran. We decided to be flattered rather than angry.

警犬
汉克历险记
〔美〕约翰 R. 埃里克森
11
HANK
EL PERRO VAQUERO
Las nuevas aventuras de Hank, el perro vaquero
2
Hank the Cowdogs eventyrlige oplevelser
JOHN R. ERICKSON
1
«بهترین سرگرمی خانواده ها در سال های اخیر» هفته نامه USA Today
کتاب پنجره
ISBN 964-92257-8-1

Part Three
Characters and Settings

The only known photograph of the historical Hank, an Australian shepherd on the Mark Mayo ranch, 1979. Photo courtesy of Stephen Mayo.

- PART THREE -

Was Hank a real dog?

Yes, there was a historical Hank, an Australian shepherd who lived on a ranch east of Forgan, Oklahoma. I knew him when I was cowboying during the Seventies, and he belonged to a neighboring rancher. The little village of Forgan has placed a granite marker on the edge of town, noting that this was the home of the original Hank the Cowdog, Mark Mayo's Australian shepherd.

The historical Hank thought of himself as Head of Ranch Security, tried to help with the cattle work, and never understood why the cowboys were always mad at him. "Hank, get out of the gate! Go to the house! Get in the pickup!" He had a good heart but wasn't very smart.

That is the short answer, but the story-Hank is a lot bigger and more complicated than the dog I knew in Oklahoma.

Was Hank based on Barney Fife?

Many readers have thought that Hank was modeled on the character played by Don Knotts in the television series "Mayberry U.S.A." I don't deny the similarity, but it didn't come from imitation. Kris and I don't own a television set and I am one of the few citizens of this country who has never seen an episode of that popular TV series.

It's hard to know what-all goes into a character, but I think Hank might show some influence from movies I've watched. My friend Paul Boller introduced me to the classic films of Laurel and Hardy, Charlie Chaplin, and the Marx Brothers, before they were widely known to my generation. Without realizing it, I became a fairly serious student of the old-time comedians.

I suspect that there are traces of Groucho Marx and Oliver Hardy in Hank's character, and I can believe that the film classics played a role in shaping the personality of Drover, Hank's sidekick—a "sawed-off, stub-tailed, chicken-hearted little mutt," to borrow Hank's description.

In the early books, I patterned Drover on a dog I knew on the LZ ranch, and I described him just as I saw him. But as the series went on, his character became more complex, and now and then, as I was writing a Drover passage, I would find myself thinking of the vacuous expression on the face of Stan Laurel, or the

Kris took this picture of the historical Drover before he became a star. In 1981 he was just a sweet little mutt on the LZ ranch south of Perryton.

dreamy, flighty, slightly insane antics of Harpo Marx.

Hank's character might have drawn some inspiration from Peter Sellers and the Pink Panther movies. I saw the first one in 1967 and have watched the sequels many times on video tape. There are parallels between Hank and the bungling French detective, Inspector Clouseau.

In the end, I don't know where Hank came from. The creative process is just as mysterious to me as it is to my readers.

Are you Hank?

When readers ask this, I always laugh and say, "I hope not! He's not very smart, you know." I'm sure that Hank and I share a few traits, and we have some of the same bad habits, but from the writing of the first story in 1981, I have thought of him as a dog, not a human in a dog suit.

I love the character and am fascinated by his contorted way of thinking. He has bought my groceries and paid off my ranch, but I'm not Hank.

How did you come up with your other characters?

In *Story Craft*, I compare the writing process to the tending of a compost heap. I throw experiences from my childhood, my work on ranches, my family, and animals who have shared my life into the compost pile, never knowing exactly what will come out of it. The characters, dialog, and plot lines that end up in my stories bear some resemblance to the experiences I've had, and to animals and people I've known, yet they've been transformed into something else.

A character is a creation of that marvelous gift we call the imagination. He or she might begin with the name, face, or mannerisms of someone I have known, but characters adapt to the needs of the story, and they seldom remain who they were in the beginning.

They seem to acquire their own identity, and when they get a call to appear in a story, they show up with their own voices and idiosyncrasies. Writers often talk about a character "running away with the story," taking a story in an entirely new direction. So let me scratch around in my memory and try to recall how I came up with the major characters in the Hank series.

Slim Chance. In the early stories, Slim was patterned on me when I was working on the LZ ranch in the years 1979-81. Like Slim, I am the kind of man who talks and sings to his dogs, plays pranks on them, and might let them stay inside the house on cold winter nights. As a bachelor in college, I had

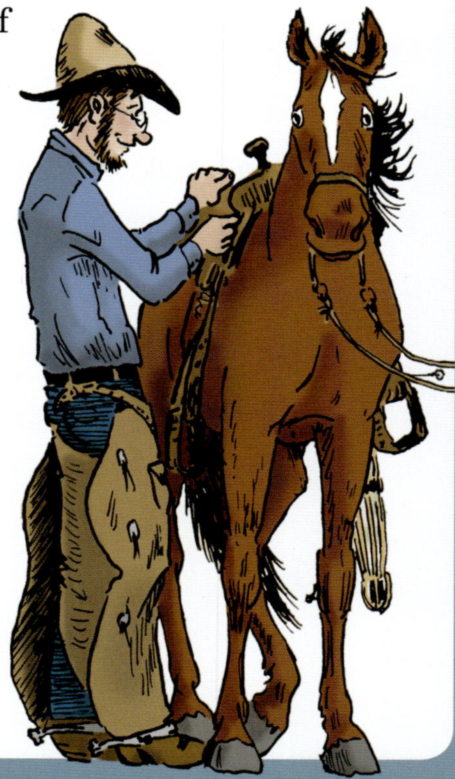

to do my own cooking and, like Slim, I had three recipes: boiled chicken gizzards, canned mackerel sandwiches, and boiled turkey necks. They were cheap and easy to fix.

Over time, I think that Slim acquired some mannerisms of three bachelor cowboys I knew and worked with during the Seventies and Eighties, Bill Ellzey, Clarence Herrington, and Frankie McWhorter, and maybe other cowboys as well. There might be a dash of Dave Nicholson thrown into the mix. Dave is a cowboy on a big ranch in Roberts County, a fine man and a good friend, and he has a slow way of talking that matches up pretty well with the way Slim talks.

Slim seems to be a composite of several men I've known, but I'm in there too. Yes, Slim and I are soul brothers.

Loper. In the early stories, Loper was based on Tom Ellzey. I was employed on his family's ranch and we worked together every day. His "handle" or nickname for our citizen's band radios was "High Loper," and that was the name I gave him in the stories.

As the series moved along, Loper grew and changed, as characters tend to do, and might have pulled in some characteristics of Tom's father, Lawrence Ellzey, who was the boss we answered to every day. But today, I don't think of Loper as either man. He has become just Loper.

Sally May. The relationship between Hank and Sally May is a gold mine of humor, one of the reasons being that Sally May understands Hank better than he understands himself.

At a glance, she knows exactly what's going through his mind: chase the cat, steal the cat's food, sneak into the yard, dig in the garden, eat a chicken, etc. Hank calls her Radar Woman because she seems to have radar for his naughty thoughts, and anytime she comes around, he begins feeling guilty.

She is a major force in Hank's life and his polar opposite. He tells us how much he wants to please her, yet much of what he does seems to make her mad. He often wonders, "What does it take to please that woman?"

In the early stories, Sally May wasn't

a major character and I thought of her as Tom Ellzey's wife Janet. That changed as the series progressed and she began taking on a likeness to my mother and wife, both of whom served as the civilizing force in a household that included children and dogs. I have gotten a lot of wonderful Sally May material, watching Kris interact with our dogs at the ranch.

I have noticed that young readers don't always understand the strained relationship between Sally May and Hank, and sometimes ask, "Why is Sally May so mean to Hank?"

Any ranch woman or mother understands: if she weren't around to impose rules of civilized behavior, the house and yard would descend into chaos. That is a level of humor that adults understand better than children, and women understand it better than men.

Drover. When I wrote the first story, my model for Drover was a little white dog on the LZ ranch, a small short-haired, stub-tailed, chicken-hearted mutt named Drover. Every day when I showed up for work at ranch headquarters, I saw him, and in the stories, I describe him just as I remember him on the ranch.

He had a sweet disposition but seemed a bit distant. He wasn't exactly unfriendly, but wasn't the kind of dog that played with children or showed a lot of affection. He never did anything wrong or got into trouble, and he was afraid of things: cattle, horses, storms, thunder, loud noises, and words delivered in a tone of anger.

When something scared him, he would vanish and hide in the machine shed. He would stay there for hours and we wouldn't see him again until he was sure it was safe to come out.

I never dreamed that Drover would

become one of the most popular, most loved characters in the series, but that is the way it has turned out. Young readers love little Drover. They think he's funny and seem to identify with his fears.

Pete the Barncat. Pete was another animal I knew on the LZ ranch, a male cat that belonged to Tom Ellzey's son Nathan. He hung out in the yard, stared out at the world, waited for scraps, and got into occasional spats with the dogs.

The actual, historical Pete wasn't a particularly vivid or strong character, but he has become a major force in the stories. He serves as Hank's arch-enemy and nemesis. Hank describes him as a dumb little ranch cat, lazy and spoiled, Sally May's rotten, pampered little pet.

Hank and Pete strike sparks the instant they see each other, and one of the problems between them is that Pete is anything *but* "a dumb little ranch cat." He is a genius at luring Hank into awkward situations. Intellectually, Pete is miles ahead of Hank, though Hank never figures it out and wouldn't admit it if he did.

Hank never seems to learn from past disasters, and one of his classic lines is, "I had the cat exactly where he wanted me." That would be a rare example of self-awareness if he understood his own words, but he doesn't.

Kids often ask if I hate cats. Absolutely not. I don't like cats the same way I like dogs, but I get along fine with our cats, and I am very fond of Pete.

He is a great character, the kind every author dreams of inventing: a villain that everyone loves to hate.

Our son Mark started listening to Hank audios when he was two years old, and grew up on Hank stories. He doesn't like Pete at all and has no patience when I argue that Pete isn't such a bad guy, but I think it's true. Pete simply plays the cards that Hank deals him. It might be annoying that he usually wins, but Hank deserves what he gets from the cat.

Little Alfred. We might say that Alfred is Every Boy, not a character that derived from any one boy in my experience. He is probably equal parts of me and our sons Scot and Mark, with a sprinkling of our grandsons, Cameron Wilson and Kale Erickson.

Alfred is a kid who has grown up on a ranch twenty-five miles out in the country. He has never lived in town. He sees other children on Sunday when the family goes to church, but the rest of the time, his best friends, his daily companions, and his playmates are adults and animals. Because he doesn't live in a place that gives him access to shopping malls, sports leagues, movie theaters, or a Dairy Queen, he has to exercise his imagination and invent his own forms of play.

That experience is common among ranch kids in the Southwest, but quite different from the experience of children who have grown up in cities.

Alfred has a special relationship with Hank, as I did with my dogs when I was young, and they are the best of friends. I have made Alfred's age somewhere between four and five years old. It's a time when he is able to talk to and understand Hank. He's not yet in school, but old enough to do some adventuring on his own.

Wallace and Junior. These two buzzards showed up in the first Hank book. If you recall, Hank has been accused of killing one of Sally May's chickens and as punishment, Loper ties the dead chicken's head around his neck with a piece of string.

Oddly enough, Hank is innocent of the crime. A coyote murdered the chicken and Hank merely ate it. On this occasion, he wasn't guilty, but he got punished anyway, and in a show of outraged dignity, he quits his job as Head of Ranch Security and leaves the ranch.

I must have thought that, after the high drama of a chicken murder, the story needed some comic relief, so I introduced a couple of buzzards who are out looking for something to eat, and catch a whiff of the chicken head. That is how Wallace and Junior entered my life, and Hank's.

My work on ranches has given me the opportunity to observe buzzards. Every year they arrive in the spring, stay through the summer months, and fly south in the fall. Every evening in the summer, they roost in the same tree, usually a big cottonwood, and every morning at daylight, they leave the roost and glide across the sky, looking for something to eat.

Buzzards are funny creatures. Not only do they have one of the worst jobs in the world, cleaning up dead animals, but they haven't been blessed with anything close to beauty. To speak bluntly, buzzards are UGLY. A buzzard has a skinny red neck, beady eyes, and a red head that is totally bald. Perched on a tree limb, his posture suggests a slouching old man with a long skinny neck.

At the time I wrote the first Hank book, I was working on the LZ ranch, which joined the ranch of the Parnell brothers, Tee and Wallace. They were old men, bachelors and gentle souls, who were still doing all their ranch work without any hired help.

One day I saw them in the pasture and stopped to chat. Wallace was in his eighties and I noticed that he had the old-man slouch of a buzzard. When I began writing the first Hank book, it just seemed appropriate to give the daddy buzzard the name Wallace.

While Wallace the Buzzard is grouchy and has an unpleasant personality, Junior is shy, friendly, and gentle, and has a "speech implement." He stutters. I don't remember why I gave him this characteristic, but I know where I got the idea. When I was growing up in Perryton, there was a boy on our block named Jimmy Gipson. He and I and Harry Drake were in the same grade, and every afternoon after school, we walked home together.

Jimmy didn't stutter all the time, but sometimes he did, and it didn't take him long to figure out that it gave him a theatrical presence. When he talked in a stutter, Harry and I laughed, so he polished his technique and developed it into a comedy routine. While trying to g-g-get out a w-w-w-word, he would spit, sputter, grunt, stomp his foot, and cross his eyes, while Harry and I sank to the ground, laughing so hard our bodies ached. Jimmy's theatrics gave me the model for Junior

At this point, we need to pause for some By-the-Way Footnotes about my buzzards.

By-the-Way #1: The proper name for these birds is "turkey vulture," but for unknown reasons, ranch people in my part of the world call them buzzards or turkey buzzards, and never use the word "vulture." I'm not sure why. Maybe our local culture regards "vulture" as too fancy, the kind of word you might hear in Austin or California, but not in the Texas Panhandle.

By-the-Way #2: I learned the technique of tying a dead chicken's head around the neck of a dog from my mother, and she learned it from her mother and grandmother, ranch women who lived near Seminole, Texas. My family has had a long history with chicken-killing dogs.

When I was a young sprout, Mother and I raised chickens in our back yard, and our beloved collie Spike sometimes succumbed to Chicken Lust. When that happened, Mother had two cures: load a chicken head with hot chili power and coax the mutt into eating it, or tie the head around his neck and let him wear it for a week. (Neither technique cured Spike of Chicken Lust).

By-the-Way #3: Several years ago, I was doing programs in a small town in Oklahoma. After the program, a mother and her son came up and told me an amazing story. They had found an abandoned buzzard nest in their barn and hatched out two eggs in an incubator. Since they were avid Hank fans, they named the chicks Wallace and Junior.

They raised the chicks into adults that roosted on the wooden fence in front of the house. The mother claimed that they were sweet and affectionate pets. This is the only instance I have encountered of people making pets of buzzards, and I am honored that they named them after my characters.

By-the-Way #4: Years ago, I was doing a reading at a bookstore in Arlington, Texas. Three people arrived during the program, and I was shocked to see Jimmy Gipson, his wife, and daughter. I stopped my reading and announced in a loud voice, "Ladies and gentlemen, it gives me great pleasure to introduce you to Junior the Buzzard!"

Jimmy blushed but was proud, and the audience thought they were in the presence of a celebrity.

Beulah the Collie. Beulah is Hank's ideal of Perfect Womanhood: graceful, warm, charming, and astonishingly beautiful. When I created the character, I had a specific dog in mind, a collie named Beulah that belonged to some friends in Beaver, Oklahoma. I remember thinking that if I were a dog, I might be attracted to a collie like her. Collies have such a nice disposition, such dreamy eyes, and such beautiful hair.

Hank dreams about her at night and often schemes about tricks and secret love potions that will draw her attention away from Plato the Bird Dog. Young readers often ask if Hank and Beulah will ever get together, if he will ever succeed in winning her heart.

I suspect not. Beulah admires what is admirable in Hank, but she is astute enough to recognize that he's a bit of a bozo. He is madly in love with Beulah until another lady dog walks past, and he loses his mind over the new girl. Hank has his charm, but in the end, he's not reliable. Most readers recognize that Beulah is right.

Plato the Bird Dog. Plato is a composite of bird dogs I have owned and observed over the years. The quality I have noticed in hunting dogs is that, while many of them are warm and affectionate, their behavior is guided by powerful instincts that involve birds and hunting. They tend to be single-minded and very professional.

That describes Plato. At the approach of bird season, he works out like a professional athlete, building his leg muscles and toughening the pads on his feet. He drills on his birding technique by pointing an old tennis shoe. He talks of little else but getting in shape and honing his skills for the opening day of bird season.

That single-minded quality makes bird dogs good at the one thing they do well (finding, pointing, and retrieving birds), but leaves them short of common sense. They tend to be scatter-brained, and one of the most often-heard refrains about bird dogs is that they wander away from home, get lost, and can't find their way back. They pick up the scent of a quail, follow it for miles, and suddenly look around and have no idea where they are.

A friend once told me she thought Plato was a parody of an ivory-tower intellectual or an absent-minded professor. There might be some truth in that, but when I created the character, I was thinking about specific bird dogs whose names I no longer remember. What I remember most is that they were all dingbats.

Rip and Snort. Anyone who lives on a ranch has observed the interaction between dogs and coyotes. It is a special relationship, like no other. Coyotes and dogs belong to the same family. Coyotes look like dogs, can bark like dogs, and sometimes they will even romp and play like dogs.

But every sensible ranch dog knows that coyotes are NOT dogs. There is something that sets them apart. The difference is almost mythological, as though coyotes stir an ancient memory in domesticated canines of a time before they were Man's Best Friend. Hank refers to them as "cannibals," because sometimes they eat dogs. (They actually do. Poodles in suburban Los Angeles are at great risk).

Ranch dogs become blasé about wild turkeys, deer, and rabbits that come close to the house, but they have a never-ending fascination with coyotes. At one time, we had two dogs, Dixie (a blue heeler) and Daisy (a yellow Lab). They slept on the front porch and when coyotes howled in the night (actually, "howling" doesn't describe the kind of hideous screaming they produce), our dogs rose from their beds and joined the chorus.

For three solid minutes, they performed an unintended satire of coyotes howling, two porch dogs, utter fools, trying to rediscover something wild and half-forgotten in their genetic past. It was hilarious, almost embarrassingly funny, a comedy routine that Laurel and Hardy never got around to doing. I often scold myself for not setting up equipment and recording one of their ridiculous sessions.

Around 1982, I read a book written by author and scholar N. Scott Momaday. He was raised in Oklahoma and descended from Kiowa Indians. He told of attending Saturday matinees when he was a boy, the kind of westerns we used to describe as "Cowboy and Indian movies."

I attended those same movies at the Ellis Theater in Perryton. Scott Momaday saw them in Lawton, Oklahoma, in a theater filled with Kiowas. In his book he talked about how the house rocked with laughter at the ways the Indians were portrayed. To them, it was comedy.

Scott Momaday gave me the original idea for my portrayal of Rip, Snort, Scraunch, and the other coyotes, and for capturing the relationship between ranch dogs

and coyotes: a parody of the corny western movies Scott Momaday and I watched as kids.

That model held through several books, but evolved into another way of viewing the coyotes. In 1987 our son Scot was in the eighth grade. He had grown up listening to the Hank audios and I had noticed that he was especially fond of the stories that involved Rip and Snort.

I remembered myself at that same age. It was an awkward time, when we were more than boys but less than men. Our bodies were starting to grow and mature, though our parents probably wondered if our brains were keeping pace.

In the eighth grade, my friends and I were loud and clumsy, proudly uncouth, and deeply self-centered. We wanted to be heroes on the football field and had suddenly discovered that half the population of our school was composed of girls. For nine months in the eighth grade, we were poised on the divide between barbarism and civilization.

It occurred to me that my coyote characters, Rip and Snort, fit that description. They have been frozen at the level of eighth grade boys, eighth grade boys forever. They are loud, violent, uncouth, and brainless. Unlike Hank, they don't have jobs or responsibilities. They sleep all day and howl all night, get into fights with badgers, roll on dead skunks to impress the women, poach a chicken now and then, and challenge their minds by engaging in belching contests.

These qualities shine forth in their songs: "Me Just a Worthless Coyote," "We Don't Give a Hoot," "Rotten Meat," and "We're Proud to be Ignoramuses." Hank is afraid of these guys (sometimes they talk about eating him), but he also admires their careless way of life. Sometimes he has fantasies about quitting his job as Head of Ranch Security, joining up with the coyotes, and becoming a cannibal.

To me, Rip and Snort are delightful characters, and very funny. I often sense, though, that mothers and schoolteachers aren't as fond of them as I am. Eighth-grade boys.

Miss Viola. My story characters are not historical figures, and often emerge as a cloud of personality traits. Sometimes I know where they came from and sometimes I don't. Viola is probably a composite of Kris and other ranch women I have known, and has grown and changed over the course of many books, but I think my original idea came from Alwilda Calliham.

When I was working on the LZ ranch in the late Seventies, Willie and her husband Glen Roy lived on a ranch on Wolf Creek, several miles east of the Ellzey's Lower Place. I used to see them at brandings and picnics.

In the late Eighties, when we moved to our ranch forty miles southeast of Perryton, Mark attended public school in Perryton, and every morning we had to drive him to a spot above the caprock to meet the school bus. The bus driver had to start her route at 4:30 or 5 every morning, rain or shine or blowing snow. That was Willie Calliham.

Viola might have begun as Willie but then grew, as characters will, into someone all her own. She has the qualities I admire in ranch women (including and especially my wife) who are brave, cheerful, resourceful, feminine, funny, kind, and full of life.

They are givers and sustainers of life, preservers of home and civilization, and always teachers. They do what needs to be done: feed a crowd of cowboys at a branding, teach a Sunday school class, nurture a sick child in the night, doctor a crippled horse, attend to a first-calf heifer, chop ice on a stock tank, feed cattle in the middle of winter, beautify her house with flowers and trees, or drive a school bus.

When Slim Chance finally gets around to noticing Miss Viola, he recognizes those qualities in her, and falls in love. How could he not?

Eddy the Rac. There is no mystery about where this character came from. In the early Nineties, we acquired an orphan raccoon and raised him to the age when he could make his own way in the wild.

This is not something I recommend that others do. It might even be a violation of state game laws. Coons are wild animals and sometimes they bite the hands that feed them, but when ranch people come across an orphan coon, bobcat, rabbit, or bird, we take them in and give them a temporary home. We know what will happen if we don't: they won't survive long in the wild.

The first thing everyone notices about baby raccoons is that they are irresistibly cute. They also adapt well and quickly to their human companions. Eddy growled at us at first, but within half an hour, he seemed content sitting on my shoulder or in Mark's lap. That seems to be an unusual quality in coons, their rapid adjustment to living with people. I wouldn't expect that in, say, baby badgers.

We kept Eddy in the house and had to figure out what to feed him. He wouldn't eat dog food or cat food, bananas or weenies, but we discovered through trial and error that he would devour green table grapes. While he lived with us, we had to keep a big supply of green grapes in the refrigerator. How a Texas coon developed such a taste for California grapes, we never figured out.

I had a feeling that Eddy would provide me with excellent story material and that I would eventually make him a character in the Hank stories. Sure enough, he made his debut in book 23, *Moonlight Madness*. He became a major character and has appeared in several books since then. Eddy is one of those characters who keep turning up in Hank's life.

The historical Eddy, our pet, introduced me to what I regard as the chief characteristic of raccoons: they seem driven to enter places where they shouldn't go, and to escape from the places

Eddy, 1991. Photo by Kris Erickson.

where they should stay. They are very intelligent and they have a pair of hands that do amazing mischief.

Eddy had a great home with us, but he was always trying to escape. One night we put him in a bathtub that had a sliding glass door. It was an enclosed space with a slick surface, and we reasoned that there was no way he could get out.

He did, and the next morning, we spent hours looking for him in the house. We didn't find him until Ashley opened a drawer in the bathroom, reached for her hairbrush, and let out a scream. Eddy was fast asleep in the drawer. How he got there we never figured out.

We bought a wire cage that was sure to hold him, and put it in the back yard. The next morning, the cage was empty and Eddy had vanished. We were living in town at that time, and knew that Eddy had signed his own death warrant. Wandering down an alley, he would run into a town dog and that would be the end of Eddy's trickery.

Then we got a call from a mechanic in the town of Booker, fifteen miles east of Perryton. He said, "By any chance, do y'all have a pet coon?" Yes. "Well, I've got him here and I'd sure like to get rid of him."

After breaking out of the cage, Eddy walked next door and crawled into the motor well of our neighbor's pickup. The neighbor drove the pickup to Booker and left it with the mechanic to get some work done on it. Eddy rode fifteen miles in the motor well of a pickup going seventy miles an hour down the highway.

The mechanic raised the hood and started working with a wrench, and was completely unnerved when he heard the engine growling at him. He jerked upright and banged his head on the hood, then got a flashlight and found Eddy perched on the frame.

We got him back, but we knew it was time for him to move along. We took him down to the ranch and turned him loose. With pet coons, you always know when it's time to tell them goodbye, and it's not as emotionally wrenching as you might expect.

In the books, Eddy is a con artist. He can do magic tricks with his hands and he has a gift for talking Hank into outrageous schemes. Hank knows that Eddy is a little crook and can't be trusted, yet he continues to fall for Eddy's schemes. *The Case of the Tricky Trap* is loaded with Eddy's con games, and Hank falls for every one of them.

Eddy is a great character and I love it when he shows up in a story.

Oh, I didn't mention how he got his name. Back in the late Eighties, we often got phone calls from a man "in Hollywood" who was determined to get the movie rights to the Hank series. He was a nice guy, but a fast-talker and a little too slick for us. We always suspected that his office

was a phone booth somewhere in Los Angeles, probably not Hollywood.

His name was Eddy. We referred to him as Fast Eddy, and when our little coon came along, it seemed an appropriate name.

Frankie the Fox. Frankie McWhorter was a ranch cowboy, horse trainer, and legendary fiddle player. I met him in 1984 when he lived on Camp Creek ranch near Lipscomb, Texas, about forty miles east Perryton. For years, we swapped out cowboy work and I wrote a book about him.

He was an extremely gifted storyteller and had an exquisite understanding of the nuances of the spoken word. I absorbed his techniques for telling a story, and his voice has been permanently imprinted on my mind. When I listen to a Hank audio in my pickup, I often think, "That's exactly the way Frankie would have said it, with a sly grin and a twinkle in his eyes."

Frankie and I were always pulling pranks on each other, and I decided to make him into the character Frankie the Fox in *The Case of the Fiddle-Playing Fox*. This scoundrel makes his living stealing eggs out of chicken houses, but not in the usual manner. He plays Bob Wills songs on his fiddle for the chickens, and the grateful old hens pay him back with fresh eggs. I considered this the ultimate cowboy prank, making Frankie McWhorter into an egg thief.

Hanging out with Frankie, I learned to imitate his distinctive way of talking, and had great fun leaving messages on his answering machine in his own voice. That was the voice I used for the fox in the audio book version of the story. I hate to brag, but I had it down cold, and some of his friends in

Lipscomb County were convinced that it was actually his voice. At his funeral, they played an excerpt from that audio book.

Frankie was a great fiddle player and worked for several years with Bob Wills and the Texas Playboys, and I was fortunate that he added his fiddle to some of the songs on the Hank audios. He was particularly fascinated by a song from *Lost in the Dark Unchanted Forest*: "Storm." It was an instrumental with me on banjo, Trev Tevis on synthesizers, and Frankie on fiddle, and we did it in the key of C-minor. I got the idea for the song listening to a Gregorian chant, and it was like nothing Frankie had ever played before. His fiddle part was haunting, sublime, beautiful.

Madame Moonshine. Again, it's hard to say where this delightful character came from, but I know that she appeared when I was reading several books in an attempt to understand Albert Einstein's Theory of Relativity. I found it hard to wrap my mind around Einstein's mathematical concepts, but one idea I retained was that things aren't always what they appear to be. Common sense doesn't always apply. Somehow, out of that came Madame Moonshine.

She made her first appearance in the second book, *The Further Adventures*. Hank had come down with a serious case of Eye-Crosserosis (he couldn't get his eyes uncrossed) and the story demanded that I find some way of getting him cured, preferably in a manner that was funny, so I invented Madame Moonshine and gave her the job.

I made her a burrowing owl, a species of bird we have on the Southern Plains. We find them in only one place, living in prairie dog holes.

They are much smaller than great horned owls and barn owls, but have the huge eyes and mysterious demeanor that are common to owls. There is something a little creepy and otherworldly about an owl's face.

Because she's a burrowing owl, she lives in a cave instead of a tree, and she shares her cave with Timothy, a large diamondback rattlesnake. As a matter of fact, burrowing owls do share space with rattlesnakes, as well as with the prairie dogs that dig the holes. All three species occupy holes in prairie dog towns, and when you walk through a prairie dog town, you need to be alert for the presence of rattlers.

Madame claims to have magic powers and she succeeds in curing Hank of Eye-Crosserosis, by giving him a ridiculous riddle to solve. He gives a ridiculous answer, and bingo, his eyes come uncrossed. Does she actually have supernatural powers? I leave that vague. Hank is convinced that she does.

She pretends to be astonished that he has solved the riddle. "Has anyone ever said that you might be a genius?" Hank, who is a master of self-delusion, admits that, yes, he hears that all the time.

Over the course of the series, Madame has made several other appearances and helps Hank overcome adversity, but we always get the feeling that she is just playing with him. Maybe she can do magic and maybe she can't, but we know for sure that she is very smart and perceptive. When she doesn't have anything better to do, she doesn't mind helping Hank out of a mess. She could do him harm if she wished, but she chooses to be his guardian angel.

Happy Lab. Happy made his first appearance in *The Case of the Perfect Dog*. He is a composite of two yellow Labs who have shared our lives on the ranch, Tango and Daisy.

Anyone who has owned a yellow Lab knows that they are the sweetest, kindest, most loveable and patient dogs on earth. At some point, usually in the first month, you begin to think that you have acquired The Perfect Dog.

That was the way we felt about Tango...until Kris laid her new iPhone

on the garden wall and began pulling weeds. When she was done, she couldn't find the phone, and Tango had vanished. She began searching and found the phone in the front yard, decorated with drool and tooth marks. Tango sat nearby, thumping her tail and looking contrite, as if to say, "Hey, I thought it was some kind of bird."

Tango survived that episode, but later had a near-death experience when Kris returned from town, set her new sewing machine down in the driveway, and carried some groceries into the house. When she returned, Tango and the nine-hundred dollar machine were missing. The dog had dragged it around to the east side of the house and crunched up the computer chips that served as its brain.

With these and other experiences serving as background material, I created the character of Happy Lab, and to me, he captures the best qualities of the breed, along with some glaring flaws.

When *The Perfect Dog* came out, Nikki Earley, who works for Maverick Books, sent a review copy to the editor of a magazine that deals exclusively with articles and stories about Labradors. We thought his readers would enjoy the book, and recognize their own dogs in Happy's character. To our surprise, he thought the book was insulting to a noble breed.

I couldn't help wondering...*has he actually lived with a Lab?*

JRE and Tango on the front porch. Photo courtesy of Lumindeo.

Where did you get the name for the town of Twitchell?

Twitchell is the setting for a number of the Hank stories, and it is based on my memories of Perryton when I was growing up. Hank's sister Maggie lives there. So do Dogpound Ralph and a couple of mutts named Buster and Muggs. The dog pound is located on the south edge of town, as it was when I was a kid, near the Isley Slaughter House. Hank calls it Devil's Island For Dogs, and he has several narrow escapes with Jimmy Joe Dogcatcher that land him in a cell at the dog pound.

Hank describes Twitchell as a huge metropolitan center, but we understand that it's actually a small town in the Texas Panhandle. It seems huge and exciting to a dog that lives on a ranch twenty-five miles out in the country. It has a wide Main Street, a couple of stoplights, and a few businesses: the Dixie Dog Drive-in, Waterhole 83, Jim's Tire Service, Foxie's Ladies Wear, and Leonard's Saddle Shop.

Hank sees many signs that say "First": First National Bank, First State Bank, First Baptist Church...etc. He concludes that Twitchell must have been the first town in Texas.

Kids in Perryton will tell you that the name "Twitchell" is an inside joke. When I was growing up, Twitchell was nothing but a railroad switch five miles east of Perryton, a place where boxcars were loaded with wheat, milo, and corn that had been stored in a big white grain elevator along the tracks.

Are any of the characters based on people in your town?

Yes, I have put Perryton friends into the books on a number of occasions. They are usually brief appearances that fit the needs of the story, and I have always assumed that the people enjoyed being mentioned. It's kind of a private joke among those of us who live in Perryton.

April and Barbara. These characters appeared in the third book, *It's a Dog's Life*. They are puppies who live in Twitchell with their mother, Hank's sister Maggie. Maggie, you might recall, isn't fond of her brother, whom she considers crude and a bad influence on the children.

When Maggie comes down with a bad headache (it happens every time Hank comes to visit), she takes a nap in her doghouse, and Uncle Hank takes the kids on a Garbage Patrol, teaching them to tip over trash barrels in the alley and pick through the garbage to find such morsels as chicken bones, fish heads, and bacon grease.

The kids have a ball with Uncle Hank and return home, reeking of garbage and scratching fleas. Maggie is furious, of course.

At the time I wrote this book, our music program at church was led by two gifted musicians, April Simpson and Barbara Richardson, and I thought it would be fun to have their names associated with pups who had picked up fleas on a garbage patrol.

Lucky for me, they thought it was funny. Barbara still directs our church choir and is now buying Hank books for her grandchildren.

J.T. Cluck. J.T. is the Head Rooster on the ranch and makes brief appearances in a number of books. People who listen to the stories on audio know that he whistles every time he pronounces an S — a speech pattern we also notice in Garrison Keillor and former President Obama.

When I came up with this character, my banker was John Tucker Cluck, president of FirstBank Southwest in Perryton. John was a dignified gentleman who usually appeared in the bank wearing a nice suit and tie. He was a member of the large and prosperous Cluck family, ranchers and farmers in neighboring Hansford County.

I thought it would be fun to honor Mr. Cluck by naming my rooster after him. I mentioned this to my father and he flinched. "John Cluck is an important man in this community, and he might not think that's funny. You'd better check with his wife."

So I called Peggy and asked her opinion. She laughed. "Oh, he would love that! Yes, do it!"

Officer Rocha. This character appeared in *The Case of the Double Bumblebee Sting*. Sally May is having a terrible day. Loper and Slim left the ranch at daylight to help at a branding, and while they're gone, Hank gets bitten by a rattlesnake. His face swells and he looks so pitiful, Sally May loads him and the children into Slim's old pickup and makes the long twenty-five mile drive into town to deliver Hank to the veterinarian.

She isn't watching her speed and gets pulled over by a highway patrolman, Officer Rocha. At that time, our highway patrolman in Perryton was Tony Rocha, a fine man and a good friend of my son Scot.

Tom Trejo. Several years ago, our favorite restaurant in Perryton was La Amistad, owned and operated by Tom Trejo and his family. Tom and his daughters waited tables and Mrs. Trejo did the cooking, and, boy, was she good! The food was delicious and it was a fine restaurant.

I became a friend of the Trejos, and found an opportunity to make Tom a character in *The Case of the Booby-Trapped Pickup*. In that story, Tom runs a donut shop and Hank plunders a load of donuts in the back of his pickup. I autographed copies of that book for Tom's grandchildren and they were proud.

Bobby Barnett. Bobby and his wife Debbie were close friends of ours until, sadly, we lost Bobby in 2015. He ran a family business on Main Street, but his first love was ranching. He ran cattle on the side and, for many years, brought his horse down to the M-Cross ranch and helped us with branding and shipping. He was always well-mounted and made a good hand.

I mentioned his name in the Hank books as often as I could, and he loved it. In *The Case of the Mysterious Voice*, a drunk driver misses a curve and crashes his pickup into Debbie's kitchen.

Doc Hardy. In *The Case of the Double Bumblebee Sting*, Hank is bitten on the nose by a rattlesnake and Sally May is so moved by his suffering, she loads him and the kids into a pickup and drives into town to the office of Dr. Ernest Hardy, DVM.

The real Doc Hardy was a longtime friend of the Erickson family and practiced veterinary medicine in a clinic on the east edge of Perryton. Any time I needed help with cattle, horses, or dogs, I took my problems to Doc. He was what you would call an old-fashioned large-animal country vet. That is, he wasn't a doggie doctor who treated house pets. He took the tough jobs involving horses and cattle that were not only messy but sometimes dangerous. He used modern medical techniques but also had a reservoir of common sense.

Doc got his medical degree at Texas A&M and was therefore spiritually welded to his beloved school. I, on the other hand, had taken my bachelor's degree at the University of Texas, for decades A&M's archrival in Southwest

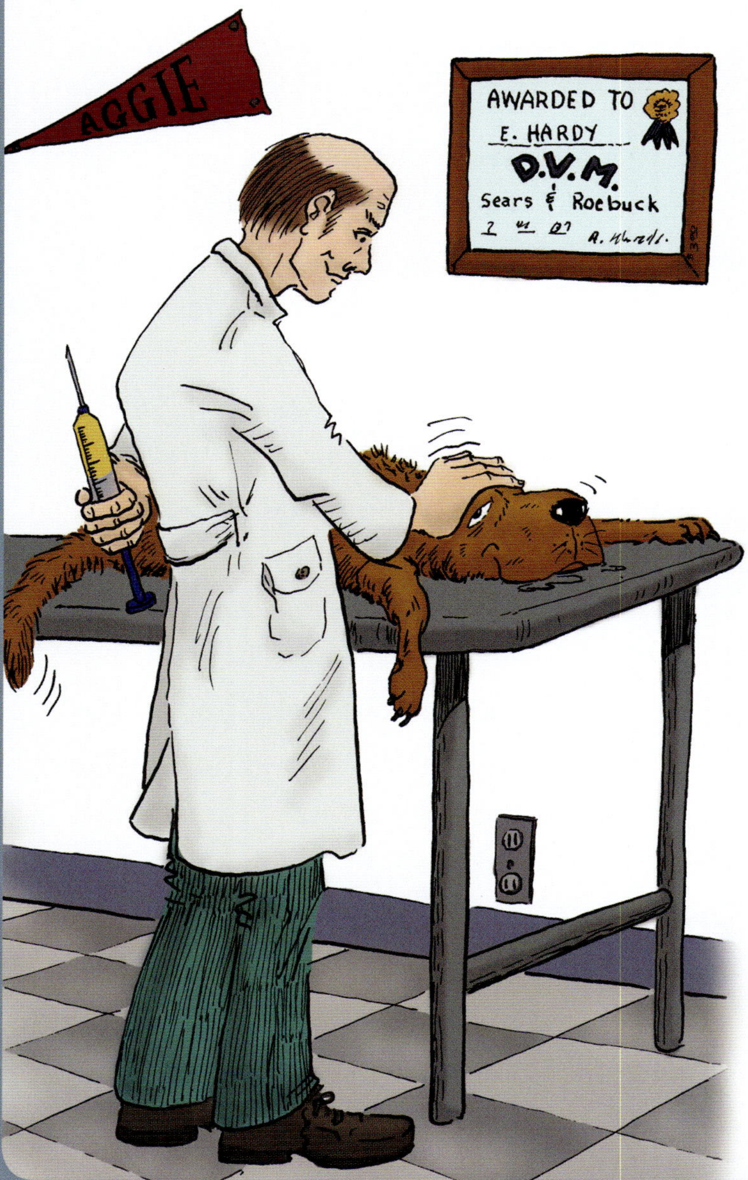

Conference football games. We tagged A&M graduates with the slur "Aggies" and they expressed their contempt for UT graduates by calling us "tea-sippers."

Neither Doc nor I actually cared about the football rivalry, but we had to keep up appearances, so we seldom passed up a chance to lob "Aggie" and "tea-sip" at each other.

One day in the fall of 1998, Doc came out to the ranch to pregnancy test my cows. I was horseback, sorting off cows in the corral with some other cowboys. Doc stood nearby, watching.

One old cow was giving me problems and wouldn't leave the pen, and when I pressed her hard on the cut, she kicked my mare in the gut. The mare jumped sideways and started bucking. I got caught off balance and hit the dirt—right in front of Doc Hardy.

A devilish gleam flashed in his eyes. He leaned toward me and muttered, "Tea-sip!"

Later, I told him that it was one of the most humbling experiences of my life, getting bucked off in front of an Aggie. Naturally, he never missed an opportunity to spread that story around town, smirching my reputation as a true man of the West.

In chapter eight of the Bumblebee story, Hank speculates that Doc Hardy might not have graduated from A&M at all, but actually bought his DVM diploma at Sears and Roebuck. That was my revenge.

Chief Deputy Kile. Bobby Kile and I go back to the very beginning of memory. We started first grade together, played football on the same Ranger team, and graduated from high school on the same night in 1962. We belonged to the same church (First Baptist), went to church camp together, and learned Bible verses in the same Sunday school classes.

As sophomores, we both played football on the junior varsity. Bobby was a running back and punter, and I played center. In the last game of the season, we were leading the other team by two points. In the fourth quarter, we had to punt. Bobby went back into the deep-snap position and called the signals. I fired the ball over his head, it rolled into the end zone, and the other team recovered for a touchdown. We lost the game.

As an adult, Bobby went into law enforcement and became chief deputy of the Ochiltree County Sheriff's Department. I recruited him as a character in *The Case of the Monkey Burglar*, and have used him many times since then. His grandchildren read about him in the Hank books and think Grandpa is a star. I think Bobby's mother would be proud of both of us.

Miguel and Jim's Tire Service. In *The Case of the Raging Rottweiler*, Slim goes to town to get a tire fixed at Jim's Tire Service. Jim's is a real business in Perryton and at the time I was writing the book, I often went there to get my tires fixed. The owner was Jim Clark who had married a girl in my graduating class, Penny Price. At one time or another, every boy in our class was in love with her. She was very sweet and pretty.

Any time I stopped at Jim's, there was a crew of men waiting to repair a damaged tire or install a new set. The foreman of the crew was Miguel Ramirez, so I made him a character in the book. He had a good sense of humor and I always enjoyed talking to him. He also had a son, Miguel Jr., who was in the same class as our son Mark and they played together on the Ranger junior varsity football team. Miguel Jr. finished medical school and is now a doctor in the Dallas area.

One day I was at Jim's, waiting for the crew to install a new set of tires on my pickup, and Jim Clark came out of the back office, carrying a poodle. I gave the pooch a pat on the head and Jim said, "Let me tell you a story about this dog."

Jim had devised a routine for the poodle. When a new customer came to the shop, Jim would say, "I'll bet you five bucks I can make this dog burp on command." An unsuspecting customer would laugh and take the bet. Jim would then open a can of Dr. Pepper and pour it into a bowl. When the dog had lapped it up, Jim would give him a shake, causing the soda to fizz in his stomach. Jim would order the dog to burp and he would burp.

Wow, I thought that was a work of genius, and of course I had to put it into a Hank book.

Ken and Sandra Splawn. Kris and I have been friends of the Splawns for decades. Ken was a coach and principal in the Perryton school system, and Sandra served many years as an elementary school teacher. They belong to our church and Sandra is a star soprano in our choir.

Sandra is a very proper lady and I have made a career out of teasing her at choir practice. My best pranks include stapling pages of her sheet music, tying a sleeve in her choir robe in a knot, and hiding her music folder. Years ago, my boys and I went to a rattlesnake roundup at Sweetwater, Texas, and I bought her a keychain made of a dried, varnished rattlesnake head. I can still hear her screams when she opened the box.

In *The Case of the Mysterious Voice*, Loper and Sally May host a big Fourth of July picnic at the ranch and invite members of the church choir. Ken and Sandra attend and Sandra brings a delicious sheet cake for dessert. Hank greets her as she's getting out of the car, and catches a whiff of the cake. Mrs. Splawn gives him the Cobra Eye and says, "Don't. You. Dare!" That is exactly the way Sandra would have said it.

Of course Hank eventually finds it, and the front cover of the book shows him standing with two feet in the middle of Mrs. Splawn's sheet cake.

Is Hank's ranch based on a certain place?

When I was cowboying full-time, I rode horseback on cowboy crews and saw a big swath of ranch country between the Canadian River in Texas and the Cimarron River in Kansas. All those sights and experiences have gone into the compost heap, but when I sit down to write a Hank book, I have a specific place in mind: the LZ ranch, 25 miles southeast of Perryton, on Wolf Creek.

I started helping the Ellzey family part-time in 1970 when Kris and I moved back to Perryton. In 1979 Lawrence offered me a full-time job, and that is where I was working when I wrote the first Hank story.

My mind holds a vivid picture of that ranch as it was between 1970 and 1981, and I know every detail of it: ranch headquarters, the ranch house, the fenced yard, the machine shed, the gas tanks where Hank and Drover have their gunny sack beds, the corrals, the cake house, the feed barn, the garden, the saddle shed, and Emerald Pond.

Slim Chance's shack is the old Dutcher house on Wolf Creek, two miles east of headquarters. I spent the night in that house on several occasions when Bill Ellzey lived there. He was a bachelor at the time, working for his Uncle Lawrence, and we amused ourselves in the evenings by shooting mice. We removed the lead from a .22 bullet and replaced it with a spit wad. With a load of gunpowder behind it, a spit wad will throttle a mouse.

The ranch where Beulah the Collie stays is the Ellzey Lower Section, about three miles east of ranch headquarters. Another couple of miles down Wolf Creek is the big old two-story house where Miss Viola lives with her aging parents. In the Seventies, it was the home of Glen Roy and Willie Calliham, and Willie still lives there today.

The Erickson M-Cross ranch in Roberts County, Texas, looking southeast toward the Canadian River.   Photo courtesy of Lumindeo.

Part Four

Studio and Stage

- PART FOUR -

Why did you decide to record the Hank stories as audio books?

From the very beginning, the Hank stories were meant to be read aloud, because the writing voice I developed imitates the oral tradition of storytelling of farm and ranch people in my area.

Electronic media has deadened the storytelling instinct in most of us, but farm and ranch people have always told stories, and they still do. When they gather at prairie fires, weddings, funerals, country dances, church dinners, farm auctions, brandings, and shipping roundups, they tell stories, and most of the time, the stories are funny.

One of the reasons humor and oral-tradition storytelling have survived in the agricultural community is that we live and work with livestock animals on a regular basis, and share our world with cats, dogs, coyotes, raccoons, skunks, buzzards, rattlesnakes, and porcupines.

Animals have their ways of leveling our best plans and teaching us humility, whether we want it or not, and those experiences make funny stories: a horse that can't be rode, a cow on the fight, a herd of yearling heifers that scatter like quail, and ranch dogs that never figure out that skunks spray, rattlesnakes bite, and porcupines have quills.

During my cowboy days, I had the opportunity to study some accomplished storytellers. I listened to their stories in branding pens, inside pickups, at kitchen tables, and horseback on long cattle drives: Ace Reid, Sandy Hagar, Glenn Green, Hobart Hall, Jake Parker, Rooster Morris, Dave Nicholson, Jason Pelham, Jim Streeter, Billy DeArmond, Jim Bussard, Jody Chisum, Lance Bussard, and Frankie McWhorter.

I studied the techniques of these oral-tradition storytellers, their timing, delivery, facial expressions, hand gestures, and regional accents, and was especially attentive to their approach to humor: the dry, subtle, understated humor of the American West. All those qualities and techniques have cropped out in the Hank stories.

When I wrote the first Hank book, the audience I had in mind was a two- or three-generation ranch family, sitting around the kitchen table on a cold winter night and reading a story aloud. I found that I could do the voices of the characters, and started doing readings for groups in Perryton. I have never had any formal training in drama, but in school, I took roles in plays and developed a little skill in acting.

By the time I had written the first book, someone suggested that I should find a company to record it as an audio

book. I found a place in Richardson, Texas, and they sent me a contract, but before I could sign it, they declared bankruptcy. I had never heard of an author recording his own book and wondered if I could do it. I counted the voices in the book: fourteen. Maybe I could push my talents to the limit and squeeze out fourteen voices.

But was there a recording studio in the Panhandle? John and Sharon Ellzey, who owned the local radio station, told me that they had done some work with a studio in Amarillo, the Audio Refinery.

I called the owner, Dayton Todd. "Have you ever recorded a book on tape?"

"Nope."

"Neither have I. You want to give it a try?"

"Sure. Come on."

In December 1982, I walked into the Audio Refinery, which at that time was located in the Avondale Shopping Center. I had two copies of the book in manuscript and gave one to Dayton. He adjusted the microphone and handed me a headset. "If you make a mistake, cough, or clear your throat, say 'edit' and keep going."

> "When I wrote the first Hank book, the audience I had in mind was a two- or three-generation ranch family, sitting around the kitchen table on a cold winter night and reading a story aloud."

I watched through a big glass window as he went into the control room, sat down in his chair, adjusted some knobs, and started his two-reel tape recorder. He gave me a nod and I began reading: "It's me again, Hank the Cowdog."

The session lasted four or five hours. Dayton stared at meters and made notes on the manuscript, but never laughed. That spooked me. When I had read aloud to an audience, they always laughed. I thought, "I have really messed this up, wasted his time and my money."

After the session, Dayton said, "That

was good."

"If it was so good, why didn't you laugh, or at least smile?"

He shrugged. "I was working. It was good." He carried two big reels of audio tape into his office. I followed and we sat down. "What do you want me to do with the production of this story?"

"Add background music and sound effects. Make it sound like a 1950s radio program."

"Got it. I've got a big library of sound effects and public domain music." At last he smiled. "I grew up a radio kid and I love old-time radio. This will be fun."

He not only loved radio, he had spent years working as a disk jockey on a local country-western station. In fact, Dayton Todd was his on-air name. His real name was Brent Herring, though as long as I knew him, everybody called him Dayton.

He went to work on the book, adding the music track and sound effects, and editing out my mistakes. In those primitive times, the editing was done with a razor blade. He physically cut and spliced the tape back together, very tedious work. In the afternoons, a student from West Texas State University came to help with the editing.

His name was Carlos Casso. A few years later, he bought the studio and has been involved in the production of every Hank audio, from the beginning, and he is very good at it.

In the spring of 1983, we brought out the first audio book in the old cassette tape format. Our children (the first audience for the tapes) enjoyed them very much, and often went to bed listening to them. Any time we drove to Garland to visit Grandma Dykema, we listened to Hank on the way. It cut down on the fighting and bloodshed in the back seat.

The tapes were harder to sell than the regular books. In the early days, a lot of people had no history of listening to books on tape, and most bookstores didn't want to carry audio books. Also, the tape sets were quite a bit more expensive than the books, but they became a popular item at public libraries. Every tape set we sold to a library got hundreds of check-outs.

I was pleased with that first audio

recording, but if I had to listen to it today, I would find it unbearable. I would hear only the flaws, the main one being my wooden delivery. In that first effort, I went into the studio and *read* the manuscript, and that's exactly how it sounded—some guy from Perryton reading a book in manuscript, in a silent, sterile room with padded walls, and wondering why the sound engineer in the other room wasn't laughing or showing any interest.

I had to figure out that my job was not to read, but to *act*. Even though I wasn't onstage, this was acting. I had to put energy and feeling into my voice, make the characters come alive, and do it in an empty room with no feedback or reward from an audience. I had to discipline myself to ignore Dayton, and later Carlos, and to ignore the customers who occasionally wandered in and stared at me through the glass.

I also learned that it was a mistake to do the entire book in a single four-hour session. It put too much strain on my voice and the strain began to show up in the last four chapters. At that point, I devised the pattern I have used ever since: I drive over to Amarillo, record the first half of the book in the afternoon, spend the night, give my voice a rest, and finish the second half the next morning.

As of today, I have recorded seventy-four books and seven shorter audio-only titles. In the Nineties, one of the stories won Best Audio Book of the Year in a competition that included Disney and the biggest publishers in the business. We have been told that Hank is the longest-running audio series in America.

Carlos Casso has done a great job of recording and producing them, and like me, he has refined his skills over the years. I think the audios we do now are quite a bit better than the ones we did in the early Eighties, though loyal Hank fans don't seem to notice the flaws in the early stories.

In 2016, a serious Hank fan in Missouri listened to every one of the audios and kept a tally on the number of characters: 153. I was shocked. I'm not an actor and was never qualified to do the audio books. I got the job because I work cheap.

Why did you start adding songs to the audiobooks?

Music has always been an important part of my life and early on, it occurred to me that songs would add another dimension to the audio books. It's something you can do in an audio that you can't do in a regular paper book.

I'm not what you would call a disciplined musician, but I've played the banjo for a lot of years, have sung in some excellent choirs, and am able to come up with musical ideas. I had never written a song until I needed one for a Hank audio, and found that I could do it.

JRE practicing a song in his office.
Photo courtesy of Nikki Earley.

The first audio had only one song, and it might be an exaggeration even to call it "music." It was Rip and Snort singing their Coyote Sacred Hymn and National Anthem, "Me Just a Worthless Coyote." They sang it off-key and without instruments.

The second book had no songs, but the third book had four: Rip and Snort redoing "Me Just a Worthless Coyote;" Junior the Buzzard singing an old folksong, "The Boys Keep Kicking My Dog Around" (I played banjo on that one); a group of cats singing "Your Momma Wears Old Tow Sack Drawers," and Hank singing "Cats Are Stupid."

I didn't know what instruments I might use on those last two songs. The day I finished recording the book, a fellow walked into the Audio Refinery. Dayton knew he was a good piano player, so right there, with no preparation, I taught him the songs and we recorded them on the spot. I don't even remember his name or if we paid him for the gig.

My little nephew, Erik Sparks, sang with me on those songs when he was just a sprout, maybe twelve years old. Later, in high school, he made All-State Choir three times as a tenor, got a degree in voice at Arizona State, and has performed with the Metropolitan Opera in New York. Nobody knows that in his youth, he got his start singing "Your Momma Wears Old Tow Sack Drawers" with his Uncle Hank.

One day when I was driving to Abilene to do school programs, I came up with an idea for a song that would fit the second book: Madame Moonshine singing "I Am a Witch." I pulled off the highway and wrote the words on a scrap of paper. Since I don't read or write music, I had to sing and hum the tune all the way to Abilene, because this was not a simple melody and I knew I would forget it. When I reached my destination, the home of Lawrence and Sonja Clayton, I borrowed their tape recorder and got it down on a cassette tape.

This song went beyond my skills on the banjo and I didn't have any ideas about finding a better musician to help me. Several weeks later, Trev Tevis played the special music at our church, a beautiful piece on the piano.

Trev was several years younger than me and we had grown up in the same church in Perryton, where his mother sang in the choir and my father played the organ. He started piano lessons at an early age, played trombone in the high school band, and became such a whiz on the marimba he made an appearance on the Ted Mack Amateur Hour.

> "Some of the Hank songs were corny and just simple fun, but we also recorded some songs that reached for genuine beauty."

After high school, he attended North Texas State University's excellent school of music, and graduated with a music degree from DePaul University in Chicago. In the Eighties, he moved back home to farm and ranch with his dad and brother.

After hearing him play the piano in church, I recruited him to work with me in the studio on "I Am a Witch" and another song I had come up with, "The Cold Weather Cowdog Blues."

Dayton Todd inserted "I Am a Witch" into the master tape of the second book, and we used "Cowdog Blues" in the fourth book. That began my long and fruitful collaboration with Trev. He took my musical ideas and made them better. Some of the Hank songs were corny and just simple fun, but we also recorded some songs that reached for genuine beauty.

I have made it standard practice to write two songs for each audio book, and have written all but three of them myself. "Followers of the Lamb" was a song we did in our church choir and I liked it so much, I found a way of putting it into *The Case of the Halloween Ghost*. We recorded it during a church service and I sang the solo. "Psalm 63" was written by a man who lives in the Homestead Heritage community near Waco. Kris and I did it as a mandolin-voice duet in *The Case of the Mysterious Voice.*

In the audio of book 71, I used a song written and performed by Mark Erickson and his band Comanche Moon. It's called "Together In This" and it deals with the experience of losing one's home in a fire, which occurs to Slim Chance in the story. Mark's song was beautiful and perfect for the story. I knew I couldn't write one better, so I asked if I could use his.

Over the years, I have brought in other musicians besides Trev. Kris has sung and played mandolin on a number of occasions, and in the past ten years, I have relied a great deal on Mark Erickson as a studio musician and arranger. Mark started singing with us when he was just a little guy. Now, as an adult, he plays standard guitar, electric guitar, bass, synthesizer, mandolin, and harmonica, and has brought in several of his musician-friends from Amarillo to help out.

Carlos Casso is a professional -quality musician and plays saxophone in the Amarillo Symphony, and he has played on several songs. His solo on "I Can See You Now" is breathtaking.

We have used the services of some of the best fiddle players in the Panhandle: Jimmy Burson, Frankie McWhorter, Rooster Morris, and Eric Chapman. Eric grew up in Amarillo and now plays violin in the Royal Philharmonic Orchestra in London. Kris and I are friends of his parents, George and Karen Chapman, and when Eric comes home for a visit, we try to lure him into the studio.

Obviously, he's a serious professional musician, and playing on our songs was a step down for him, but he had a great time doing them.

JRE and Carlos Casso, recording an audio book in the Audio Refinery. Photo by Kris Erickson.

Do you have a favorite song?

Since 1982, we have recorded more than 140 songs, and they cover a wide range of moods and styles. It would be hard for me to pick one favorite, so let me mention several.

"I'm Rich," book 7: We don't play a lot of Bluegrass-type songs, but this one clearly comes from that tradition. It features me on banjo, Kris on mandolin, Trev on synthesizers, and Frankie McWhorter on fiddle. It's a bouncy song with a strong beat, and it's a good one for closing a program. It leaves the audience upbeat and smiling.

"Storm," book 8: This is one of the few instrument-only songs we've done over the years, and it was meant to capture the drama of a thunderstorm. I got the idea after listening to Gregorian chant, an ancient form of church music. Trev played synthesizers and marimba, and Frankie McWhorter added a nice part on the fiddle. Frankie used to play in Bob Wills' band, and was fascinated by this song, because it was so different from anything he had ever played before.

"Silly Old Maid," *The Dancing Cowboy*: This is a simple song that accomplishes more than I ever expected. I got the idea for it one morning when I was walking to my office before daylight. It uses only three chords and the words are nothing special, but somehow it shines as a song. Kris, Mark, and I played our instruments on the recording, and Kris and I did the vocals.

"Gloria," book 20: I must have gotten the idea for this one in church, because it definitely shows my affection for classical sacred music. The words come from the Latin mass and that's pretty unusual, a Latin text in a book narrated by a dog. We recorded it as a children's choir, using the sweet little voices of our children, Ashley and Mark, doubled and tripled on a sixteen-track tape. Trev added a nice piano part.

"Rotten Meat," book 5: This is one of several coyote songs that appear in the audios. As a musical experience, it's not much. When I played the final mix for my father, a good musician, he buried his face in his hands and moaned, "John, that's terrible!" But oddly enough, it has always been a favorite at my performances. It makes people laugh, so what it lacks in musical sophistication, it makes up in showmanship. An audience often remembers songs that a real musician would rather forget.

"Ridiculous Things," book 59: I like this one for several reasons: it has a nice combination of chords, I did a good job on the lyrics, and I have always liked the character who sang it, Happy Lab. For me, the song captures all the qualities we love and don't love in a Lab. Kris, Mark, and I did the instrumentals.

"Another Cowboy Day," book 19: This might be the most musically complex song I ever came up with. It starts in the key of C, goes to D#, then transitions back into C, and it uses several minor chords along the way. I can't explain why it turned out as it did or why the different keys work well together, but they do. I also like the text, a cowboy explaining his love for the cowboy life.

John, Kris and Trev Tevis performing in 1984.

"My Heart Goes Wild For You," book 7: This is a back-and-forth love song between Hank and Missy Coyote. Trev did a great job of arranging and playing synthesizers and marimba, and the song shows off Kris's beautiful soprano voice.

"Our Song," book 68. This is another instrumental. It started with a set of chords I was playing on the banjo. Kris said she liked it and thought I should make it into a song, so I worked it into the audio version of book 68, a love song that appears when Hank sees Beulah. I turned the arrangement over to Mark and love the way he worked in electric guitar and dobro. I never get tired of listening to it. As my father once said about one of my songs, "That's real music."

Why did you start doing programs in schools?

In the early years, 1982-1984, I started doing programs as an after-dinner speaker for groups that had some connection to agriculture, such as Farm Bureau, banks, cattle feeders, grain farmers, dairy farmers, and even shrimpers down on the Gulf Coast. Most of these programs were a long way from home and I was flying off to Montana, Iowa, Kansas, Nebraska, and Canada to do them.

I was reading Hank to those audiences and there were never any children in the room. The stories worked great on these adults, which added to my perception that they were not meant for children. A program I did for the Western Barley Growers of Canada in Banff, Alberta, was especially raucous. These farmers were consuming their own product, barley, in the form of beer, and by the time I did the program, they would have laughed if I'd been reading from the book of Leviticus.

In the late 1990s, I was one of six authors invited to a literary gala put on by the Friends of the San Antonio Public Library. It was a major event that drew a full-house crowd of 600 people, and the celebrity author of the evening was Steve Allen, who hosted a popular television show in the fifties and sixties. He had just brought out a new book.

Each author was given ten minutes

to speak. I was fifth on the list and the organizers gave the final slot to the headliner, Steve Allen. We all sat at the head table, facing the audience. Mr. Allen was up in years, maybe in his eighties, and he very conspicuously fell asleep during the first author's presentation.

He awoke long enough to give polite applause when the author sat down, then went right back to sleep, and the pattern continued through four authors' presentations. I suspect that the people who hired him were concerned.

I went to the platform and read the Poisoned Weenies chapter from *The Case of the Midnight Rustler,* where Hank devours a whole package of weenies while Slim Chance is occupied with other matters. During the reading, while Hank is gorging himself, I read with my mouth stuffed with bread. It made my voice sound ridiculous and I was spraying breadcrumbs into the air.

Steve Allen sat directly to my left. At first, he stared at me in disbelief—"Is this guy crazy?"—then cackled until tears rolled down his cheeks. He didn't sleep a wink during my reading and I'm sure the organizers of the event were relieved. After the program, he came up and pumped my arm. "You ought to record that stuff on tape!" I confessed that I already had. I think my dad would have been proud that Steve Allen stayed awake during my reading.

Like so many of the things that have happened to me over the years, performing in schools just dropped out of the sky. One day in 1984, I got a call from Vicki May, who was the elementary school librarian in Spearman, a little town west of Perryton. She asked if I would do a Hank program for her kids. I told her, "I can do the program, but I don't think children will understand the humor. It's pretty subtle. I wrote those books for adults."

She said, "They're bringing the books to school and reading them on their own. They're laughing. They think they understand the humor."

I did the program for three hundred children in the gymnasium, and sure enough, they laughed and enjoyed it. At that point, we started putting out the word among teachers and librarians that I was available to do school programs, and we got a good response. I started visiting schools in the Panhandle and gradually the circle began to widen, and before long, I wasn't doing any more after-dinner programs for adults.

The banquet speaking was a good source of income, but performing in schools fit me better. Not only did I enjoy working side-by-side with teachers and librarians (among the best, most dedicated people on earth), but I shared their passion for literacy—introducing school kids to the joys of reading. Now, that was important work!

Until 1986, the Hank books were not well known outside of ranching communities in West Texas, New Mexico, Oklahoma, and Kansas. Then I was invited to speak to a librarians' conference at Sam Houston State University in Huntsville. I did a program of Hank songs and readings for a thousand librarians from Dallas, Houston, Austin, and San Antonio.

It was my good fortune that the speaker before me had a doctorate in some arcane subject, and delivered a speech that was so dull, flies were dropping dead all over the auditorium. My presentation brought the crowd back to life and I had the librarians laughing and clapping. We had a rip-roaring good time, and after the program, they stampeded into the lobby, bought Hank books, and took them back to their schools.

Before long, I was doing school programs far from home, and Trev Tevis started traveling with me on road trips. Sometimes we headed north to Indiana, Kansas, Colorado, Nebraska, or Wyoming, but most often our destinations lay to the south. Texas is a huge state with thousands of schools. All of them are south of Perryton and most of the ones we visited were in the Houston area, along the Texas Gulf coast, or in East Texas—a long drive from home.

When we left Perryton on a two-week road trip, we had a foam mattress in the back of the Suburban and pulled a four-wheel covered trailer that was packed tight with boxes of Hank books, as well as Trev's marimba, two synthesizers, two big speakers, and a heavy control board.

On a typical trip, we took turns driving and sleeping and arrived in Houston twelve hours later. We performed in suburban schools (Katy, Spring, Humble, Cypress-Fairbanks, The Woodlands, Conroe, and others) and worked our way north into East Texas, which had more little towns and eager Hank fans than I had ever imagined.

ReAnna Wilson reading a great literary work to Daisy at the ranch. We lost this precious granddaughter in a tragic accident in 2017. She was only 13, had begun performing with us and loved 'Silly Old Maid.' Photo by Nikki Earley.

At every stop, we had to unload boxes of books and, in effect, set up a portable bookstore, then set up the stage with Trev's marimba, keyboards, synthesizers, and speakers. Sometimes we performed in an auditorium, but more often we set up in the school cafeteria or gymnasium. After the programs, we loaded up and drove to the next destination. We often drove into the night and stayed in the homes of teachers and librarians.

In the early years, we did four programs a day, and in large school districts, that meant we were setting up and breaking down at four different schools. It was exhausting work. When I got back home from a road trip,

I would sleep for two days straight. We kept up that pace for years, until I realized that I wasn't having fun any more and dreaded going out on the road. I cut back the number of programs to two per day, raised my fee, and made fewer trips.

We always ended our programs with a raucous coyote song called "Daddy Packed His Suitcase 'Cause Momma Was a Mean Old Bag." In the middle of the song, Trev rose from his keyboard and played a trombone solo, but this was no ordinary piece of trombone work. Trev played it loud and *badly*, which was something he had never thought of doing until he started working with me.

We called it "Coyote Trombone"—piercing, off-key, out-of-tune blasts that had a stunning effect on the audience. At first, they couldn't believe what they were hearing, then they burst out laughing.

After doing this for several years, Trev refined his technique, loading the bell of the trombone with talcum powder. He showered the first five rows with a cloud of white dust and created the impression that his trombone had caught fire.

That song might have brought American music to a low point, but it was a fine piece of showmanship and a great way to end a program. On several occasions, the music teacher came loping up after the program and told Trev, "You must be pretty good to play *that* badly!"

"It was a slow but honest way of building an audience. . . . We built a relationship of trust, and now we're selling books to a second generation of Hank readers."

We built the Hank franchise, not with advertising, but with school programs, most of them in small towns. It was a slow but honest way of building an audience. I entertained them and signed their books. I met the parents and had lunch with the teachers and librarians. We built a relationship of trust, and now we're selling books to a second generation of Hank readers.

How far from home have your appearances taken you?

To the east, Savannah, Georgia, and Harrisburg, Pennsylvania. To the South, Brownville, Texas, and Key West, Florida. To the west, San Diego, California, and Everett, Washington. To the north, Canada and Alaska.

Trev and I made the Alaska trip in January1988. We flew from Amarillo to Dallas, changed planes, flew to Seattle, changed planes, flew to Anchorage, changed planes, and flew to Kenai. It was the longest plane trip I'd ever made and it didn't make me want to visit China or Australia.

Most people avoid Alaska in January, but it's a big month for bookstores and libraries. Because the days are so short and the weather so cold, Alaskans do a lot of reading in the winter. It seemed that half the citizens of Alaska were born in Texas, and they bought a slug of Hank books.

We spent a week doing school programs on the Kenai Peninsula (a recent volcanic eruption had left a layer of gray ash on everything), then flew north and spent another week in Fairbanks. The week we were there, the high temperature was zero, but the cold didn't bother me. In fact, it seemed more pleasant than the kind of wind-driven cold we had in the Panhandle. The week we were there, Fairbanks had no wind. The steam plume from a power plant rose straight up.

I was reminded of an old joke. Two men in Alaska are dressed in parkas and looking at a thermometer that shows thirty below zero. One says, "Boy, don't you know it's cold in Amarillo!" There is a lot of truth in that.

We attended a dog sled race and ate a lot of salmon and moose, no beef. I was surprised to learn that Alaska has no cattle. All their beef has to be shipped in, and moose is a staple in the diet. We saw a lot of moose. One day I was talking to a class of students and looked out the window. Several moose were standing in the school yard, staring at me. School officials had to be alert to the presence of moose because they are very large animals and sometimes aggressive.

Do you get nervous before a performance?

It's odd, but I have never gotten "butterflies" before a program. The Hank material is so natural to me, I don't worry about it because I'm not pretending to be anything other than what I am. I'm John Erickson, a pretty good banjo player, a pretty good singer, and a pretty good actor. I don't pretend to be a star or a headline performer, or want to be.

It helps that I've written a series of books that the people in the audience already know and have enjoyed. An audience that might hold a professional musician or actor to a high standard will allow an author to make mistakes. If I forget the words to a song or if my banjo is a bit out of tune, my audience doesn't care. The only thing they

Kris's Nugget mandolin and John's Stelling Staghorn banjo, both fine instruments.

might not forgive would be dishonesty.

The size of the audience doesn't bother me. I do the same kind of presentation whether it's in a big auditorium or a school library. I enjoy the bigger venues because the sound system is always top quality and the acoustics are good. In a big auditorium, you really can't see the hundreds of people out there in the seats. The house lights are down and the stage lights are bright, leaving you mostly blind.

I've performed in some great facilities in Sulfur Springs and Orange, Texas; Ponca City, Oklahoma; Lubbock's Civic Center Auditorium; the George H. W. Bush Presidential Museum; A&M Corpus Christi's auditorium; Amarillo's Globe News Center; and the MGM Grand Hotel in Las Vegas.

Those auditoriums seat between 600 and 2500 people, the MGM Grand being the largest. Kris, Mark, and I performed there for the International Reading Association. The auditorium was so large, they had big television screens above us that showed the performance. I must admit, that spooked me at first.

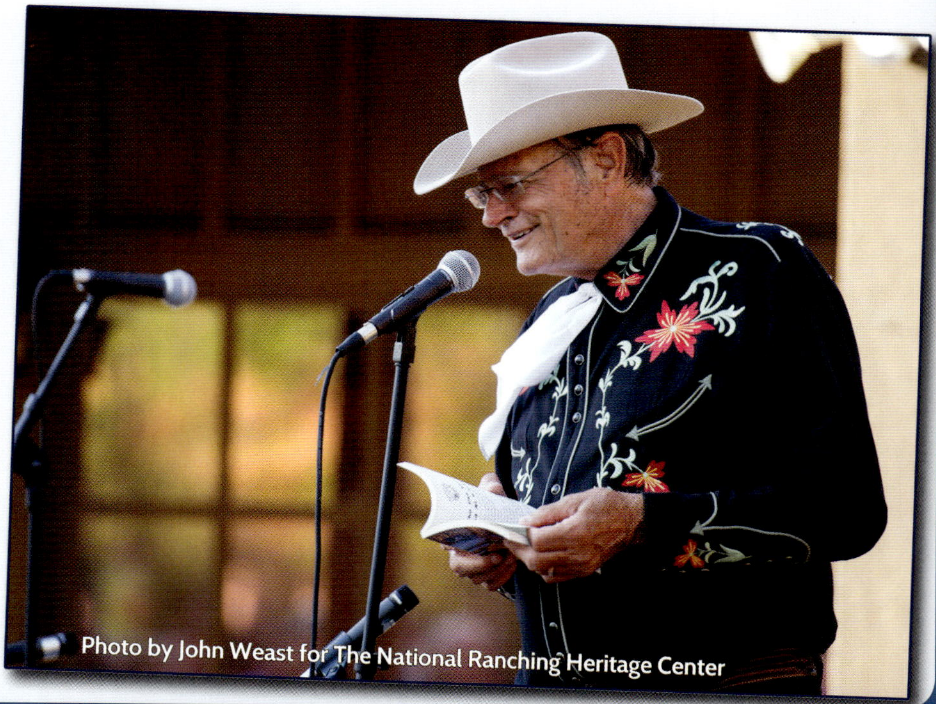

When and why did you start writing Hank stage plays?

One of the things that make the Hank stories unique is that they are a natural performance medium. Most books are just books, ink and paper between cardboard covers, and they don't translate well into the spoken medium. If you try to read them aloud to an audience, people start falling asleep. If you doubt that, try reading a Dostoyevsky book aloud to an audience.

The Hank books are different because, from the start, they were meant to be read aloud, performed. I built my audience, not with advertising, but by reading aloud to an audience. From there, it was a short step to do them as audio books and performances in schools, and bringing in music. Stage plays were a short step beyond the one-man shows I do in schools. The main difference was that I invited other actors to share in the fun I was having, doing the whole thing by myself.

I don't remember when I started writing the stage plays, years ago, probably in the late 1980s or 1990s, and I might have gotten the idea from a fellow named Larry Patton who taught theater classes at Butler County Community College in Eldorado, Kansas. He asked if he and his wife Vicki could pull scenes, dialog, and characters from the Hank books and turn them into a musical play. They did, and invited me to attend the first performance. It was very good.

A few years later, Mrs. Simpson, the theater teacher at Perryton High School, did something similar, only with high school kids, and it was a wonderful show. At that point, I started writing my own plays.

Cast of the Perryton High School Hank play with John Erickson, 2003

I did revisions of the two plays that had been done and wrote four or five on my own. In typical fashion, Gary Rinker and I didn't know what to do with them. Gary is a whiz with numbers and I'm a pretty good wordsmith, but neither of us is very good at marketing. But somehow word got around, and the plays were produced in Arlington, Plano, Round Rock, Snyder, Houston, and Amarillo, Texas; Tulsa, Oklahoma City, and Asheville, North Carolina.

Main Street Theater in Houston did a Hank play as a traveling show and performed it in a hundred schools. Two years later, they did another one.

Several years ago, Gary got a call from someone in China. They wanted to hire a writer to adapt the first Hank book into a play. Gary told them I wanted the first shot at it and wrote the script in two weeks. They were pleased with my version and it played over the summer in a theater in Beijing. I kind of wish I could have seen it, but I'm chilled at the thought of spending sixteen hours cooped up in an airplane.

I had a natural affinity for theater and took lead roles in plays in high school, but I'm not what you would call a theater person, someone who is passionate about producing, directing, or acting in a play, someone who loves the smell of grease paint and the roar of the crowd. People who excel in that medium would rather be in a theater than anywhere else. I would rather be at home on my ranch, so I will always be an amateur thespian. I'm also an amateur singer, banjo player, composer, poet, screenwriter, scholar, and archeologist. I love being an amateur.

The Chinese stage production, photos courtesy of Beijing Hua Yi Culture Media Co., Ltd.

Part Five

Personal Questions

Photo by Nathan Dahlstrom.

- PART FIVE -

How did the wildfire of 2017 affect your writing?

On the afternoon of March 6, 2017, strong wind damaged a power line on a ranch that joined us on the northwest. It started a prairie fire that authorities called the "Perryton Fire," which burned 318,000 acres in four Panhandle counties. It has been listed as the third-largest wildfire in Texas history.

Kris and I were able to evacuate and drove to Perryton. The fire destroyed 90% of the pasture on our place, as well as our home, a guest house, and my writing office. We left with the clothes we were wearing, our two Mac laptops, and Kris's Nugget mandolin. My computer held the files of five unpublished Hank books, as well as this book, but we lost all our other possessions, including two concert-quality Stelling banjos and a good friend, Dixie, our blue heeler.

For the next four months, we lived in a small duplex in town, and my regular morning writing routine was, to put it mildly, interrupted. After spending a few days in limbo, I restarted my discipline of rising early, and began writing a few hours every morning in Gary Rinker's office at the Maverick Books warehouse, before I had to drive 40 miles to the ranch to feed cattle. They had nothing to eat after the fire.

I kept notes about my life at the time: the fire, how it affected our lives, and what I was doing every day on the ranch. It became a classic case of...when Life gives you lemons, you make lemonade. An author writes about what he sees, knows, and feels, and the fire provided me with plenty of material, though not exactly what I would have chosen.

I kept detailed journal notes, which is something I had done during the wildfire of 2006, and at some point, it occurred to me that in the span of eleven years, I had been an eyewitness to two of the biggest wildfires in Texas history. I decided to combine my observations and thoughts of the two events, and turned it into a nonfiction book about wildfires.

I finished the fire book in June 2018 and submitted it to a university press for their consideration. The response of the editors was positive, and they have sent the manuscript to "readers" to get their opinions. If the book makes its way through the approval process, we might see it in published form in the next year or two.

Sometime around the middle of April, my sons, Scot and Mark, found a portable building near Amarillo that would make a good replacement for the office that had burned, moved it to the ranch, and hooked it up to water and electricity. I began driving to the ranch before daylight, commuting to the office, you might say, with a new friend, Rosie. She was a red heeler pup that Scot gave me to replace Dixie.

In June, I plunged into the writing of a new Hank book. After the fire, I worried that, with my life and routines in such a jumbled state, Hank might have gotten lost, and that when I knocked on his door, he might not show up.

Even though I have been writing Hank books for 35 years, I have never known if he would answer my knock.

But he did, and of course the new adventure was about a wildfire that sweeps across Hank's ranch. I finished it in three weeks and thought it might be good enough to put into the lineup of Hank books, without letting it sit for the usual three years. My editors, Kris and Nikki Earley, agreed, and we brought it out in the spring of 2018: *The Case of the Monster Fire*.

The audiobook version of the story included a song called "Together In This," written and performed by our son, Mark. He wrote it two years before our fire, but it has an eerie resonance of the events we experienced in 2017.

In August, Kris and I moved into a new double-wide home on the ranch, and we are getting our lives back into something close to what they were before the fire. I have a nice little office to work in and a fine little dog to chase bugs on the porch at 5:30 in the morning, but I lost my entire library of books about Texas history, church history, theology, ancient Egypt, and Panhandle archeology. I also lost all the journal books I began keeping in 1968, and all my correspondence with Elmer Kelton, John Graves, and other writers.

Those items can't be replaced, and it's hard to comprehend the loss of a library, but as Job said, "Naked I came into this world, and naked I will leave it." We move on.

After the fire. Photos by Nathan Dahlstrom.

Do you write any other books besides Hank?

Yes. As I mentioned, I write every day and can't write Hank books all the time, so I have to find other things to do. I have probably written eight hundred articles that were published in newspapers and magazines, and have published twenty-three non-Hank titles. (In case you're interested, I've listed them all in the Appendix).

The University of North Texas Press has brought out six of my nonfiction books in their Western Life Series. These are books about ranch-related subjects, good, solid books based on my experiences as a cowboy during the Seventies and Eighties. In my humble opinion, *Catch Rope* and *The Modern Cowboy* give as honest and accurate an account of cowboy life and work as you will find in the literature of the West.

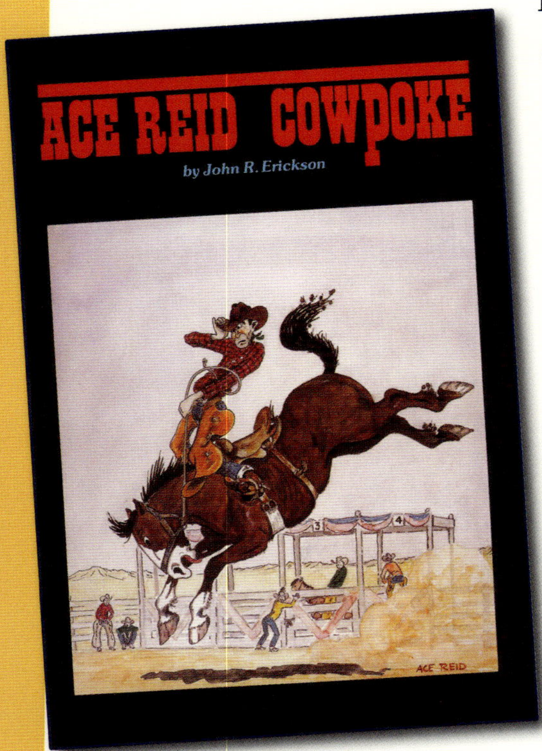

I also have written a three-book series of novels about a character named Riley McDaniels. He lives on a Texas ranch with his widowed mother and brother during the years of Prohibition in the 1920s. I published a five-book series of short humorous sketches about cowboy life, including *The Devil in Texas and Other Cowboy Tales*, where Hank made his first appearance in a short story.

These are all good books and I'm proud of them, but they live in Hank's

Photo by Kris Erickson.

shadow. They sell very few copies and most people don't even know they exist. My audience wants me to write Hank books, period. I wish the other books were better known, but Hank steals the show. That it's a nice problem to have. Most authors would love to have it.

Arthur Conan Doyle had the same problem with Sherlock Holmes. He considered his long scholarly history of the Boer War to be his finest piece of work, but his audience wasn't interested in the Boer War and wanted more Sherlock Holmes stories.

Conan Doyle came to dislike his famous character and even quit writing Sherlock Holmes stories, but his audience made him go back to them. I am fortunate that I love writing Hank. I just can't do it every day of the year.

What are your hobbies?

On both sides of my family, I come from people who didn't know much about what we call "having fun." Their lives were shaped by home, family, church, and work, and that's where they put most of their time and energy. My mother and father never took a vacation. I have followed a similar pattern.

I don't play golf or tennis. We don't have a television, so I don't get many opportunities to watch football, basketball, or baseball. My sons and I do some hunting on the ranch (deer, turkey, quail, and dove), and before the drought dried up our pond, I enjoyed catching bass and perch with my kids and grandchildren. We always cook what we catch and shoot. I enjoy the eating as much as the hunting.

Photo by Doug Boyd

I suppose I could call my interest in archeology a hobby, although if you dabble deeply enough in archeology, it begins to resemble Hard Work. I became interested in Texas Panhandle archeology in 1990 when we bought our ranch in Roberts County. We had several of the kind of sites that arrowhead hunters look for: a scatter of cultural material (flint flakes, bone, ash, and pieces of pottery) on the surface, usually near an active spring.

I wanted to be a good steward of these sites and to learn as much as I could about the people who lived on my ranch centuries before I arrived. I began reading books and articles about local archeology, and made the acquaintance of some people who shared my curiosity and knew a great deal more than I did. In 2000 we began a series of controlled scientific excavations that have added to our knowledge of the prehistoric people who occupied this region between 1250-1450 A.D.

I am very fortunate that I love my work as an author and rancher. I don't want to go on vacations because if you love what you're doing, every day is a vacation. I also love the home Kris has made for us. We go to town when we must and enjoy doing things around the house the rest of the time.

Kris is an excellent cook and enjoys gardening and keeping a beautiful yard. She does photography, makes scrapbooks, and is a very good quilter. I always have a stack of magazines to read when I'm in the house, and I spend a lot of time writing and answering emails, including many from Hank fans. Neither Kris nor I have developed an interest in social media.

Music is an important part of our lives. We have sung in our Methodist church choir since 1979 (Kris sings soprano, I'm a tenor). We have an excellent choir director in Barbara Johnson. We do difficult music that requires serious rehearsal time, and I would say there aren't many small town churches that can deliver a Christmas or Easter cantata better than we can.

Quilt and photo by Kris Erickson

We also sing in a community choir that does Handel's "Messiah" every year at Christmas time. Perryton has been doing "Messiah" for sixty-three years, which is a remarkable accomplishment for a small community, because it's a very demanding piece of music. Most of our soloists are local people and we bring in a string ensemble from the Amarillo Symphony.

Kris and I spend time in the evenings playing our instruments, mandolin and banjo. The musical side of Hank has given us the opportunity to perform together on stage and in the recording studio. Kris doesn't travel with me all the time, but when I have a program fairly close to home, she enjoys performing and, naturally, her charm and talent add a lot to the performance. I think people in the audience enjoy seeing a husband and wife working together.

We don't practice as often as we should, and certainly not as much as serious musicians do, but we try to keep up our skills. Fingers get rusty and slow without practice, and we have to remember the words to twenty-five or thirty songs. When Mark comes to visit, he brings his Taylor guitar and plays with us. He started performing onstage with us when he was four years old.

Here's another thing Kris and I do: we talk to each other. That might sound odd, but pastors and marriage counselors remind us that a lot of busy couples today *don't* talk to each other, and it creates problems for a marriage. We have always regarded our marriage as our most important asset and have spent a lot of time keeping it strong.

In August 2017, we celebrated our fiftieth wedding anniversary, so apparently we've done some things right.

JRE, Bobby Barnett and Nathan Dahlstrom
Photo by Kris Erickson

Is it fun, being an author?

In some respects, being an author is like being anything else: a lawyer, doctor, minister, schoolteacher, farmer, or plumber. You go to your job every day, put in your time, and try to do honest work. You have good days and bad days, great days and days when you wonder why you ever got into this mess.

But in other ways, being an author is unique. It's not one of the standard professions that offer stability and security, such as you would find as an accountant, computer engineer, or nurse. Writing falls on the creative side of things, and it offers some of the joys and uncertainties known to actors, painters, filmmakers, and musicians.

Creative people don't go into their professions because it's the smart, safe thing to do, or because it will guarantee them a nice home in the suburbs. I suspect that most of them are led, driven, or called by forces that are not totally rational. It's something they feel they *have* to do, come what may.

My first fifteen years as a disciplined writer involved a lot of hard work and very little reward. I wrote four hours a day, seven days a week in the morning, then went to a "real" job to support my family. I was sending out manuscripts and query letters to magazines and book publishers, and mostly getting rejection slips back in the mail.

My total income for those fifteen years probably came to $3,000. Let's look at the numbers.

4 hours x 7 days x 52 weeks x 15 years

The author loafing with his dogs, Dixie and Daisy. Photo by Nathan Dahlstrom.

= 21,840 hours = $00.1373 per hour.

Thirteen cents an hour for fifteen years! What kind of dunce would go into such a profession? I could have been making five bucks an hour working at any minimum wage job.

During those years, I enjoyed the creative process, developing my natural talent and stringing words together on a page, but the rest of it wasn't much fun. I was constantly worried about money, and my spirit was battered every time I received a rejection slip—and I probably got close to a thousand of them.

That began to change when Hank walked into my life (a complete surprise) and I discovered what I was supposed to be doing with my talents. I self-published the books, went out and found an audience, and began making more than thirteen cents an hour for my time.

Photo by Kris Erickson

Photo courtesy of Lumindeo.

It has turned out much better than if I had planned it myself, and I can say that being an author is a lot more fun today than it was back then. I'm doing work that has meaning. I'm invited to do Hank programs and spend time with high-quality people. I'm giving kids and families the gift of innocent laughter and introducing children to the joy of reading. I get a lot of wonderful fan mail and sign so many books my hand aches. I meet parents who appreciate what I do, and kids who say they love my books.

That's a great reward, even if it took a while.

I still go through periods when I don't have ideas or inspiration, but I expect that. It has happened before and I will work through it. We can't eat ice cream all the time.

Do you have a family?

Kris and I have been married since 1967, and we have three children: Scot (1974), Ashley (1978), and Mark (1982).

Scot is married to Tina. They live in Amarillo and have four children: Kale, Alyssa, Savannah, and Sawyer. Scot is a dirt contractor and runs the kind of heavy equipment little boys dream of operating: graders, dozers, trackhoes, backhoes, skid loaders, and big diesel trucks. The first time he ever sat down on a backhoe, he was able to run it.

Ashley is married to Randy Wilson and works in retail. Randy is a skilled carpenter and is one of those fellows who can do almost anything with his hands and a set of tools. They raised two children in Canadian and Cameron played on the state championship football team in 2016. We lost ReAnna in a tragic accident in 2017. She was thirteen, a bright spirit and a wonderful girl. Kris taught her to cook, sew, quilt, and play the mandolin. We cherish her memory.

Mark graduated from Texas State University and Texas Tech School of Law. He has a private law practice in Amarillo and has taken a leading role in HTC Productions.

He is an accomplished musician, singer, songwriter, arranger, and performer, and is lead singer for the band Comanche Moon. He has played with me on a number of Hank songs that appear in the audio books and does all my arrangements.

John, Kris, Mark, Scot, and Ashley, 1984.

Does your wife help you with your writing?

Sometimes when Kris and I are doing a program together, I tell the audience, "If you love these stories, you ought to give Kris a big hug, because without her, you wouldn't have any Hank books."

Kris doesn't go with me to my writing office every morning or give me a flood of story ideas, but her spirit and personality are present in every story, like oxygen in a room. You don't see it or hear it, but if it weren't there, life would cease. She gives life and meaning to my efforts as a writer.

From the very beginning, she saw that I had a gift for writing and encouraged me to use and develop it, even during the years when my writing wasn't all that good

Photo by Doug Boyd

and I was getting a flood of rejection slips from publishers. She did without nice clothes and nice cars while I was learning my craft, and followed me to isolated ranches while I was working as a cowboy.

When I needed a photographer to illustrate my magazine articles and nonfiction books, she bought a camera and some books, took a few classes,

and learned photography. She even developed her own black and white prints in a homemade darkroom.

When I needed an intelligent reader to give me an honest opinion about a piece of writing, she became my editor and had the thankless job of saying, “This might not be as good as you thought.”

When we started Maverick Books, she wasn’t frightened that we were taking on debt and might not be able to repay the note at the bank. Somehow she knew we would.

When I started writing songs, doing performances, and recording music for the audios, she bought a mandolin and a chord book and began playing with me, and contributed her pure soprano voice to the songs.

Around and between all of that, she created a warm, loving home for me and our children, provided us with nourishing meals, and gave us an example of a strong, wise, godly woman.

Kris has the amazing gift of making the people around her *better*. She has made me a better man and a better writer. She’s in every Hank book, like the oxygen you’re breathing.

Kris in her home. Photos courtesy Lumindeo.

Will there ever be a Hank movie or TV series?

Well, that's a long story. In 1984, when we had brought out four Hank books, I got a call from a director at CBS Television. He wanted to adapt the first book into a 30-minute animated episode in the network's series "CBS Story Break."

Kris and I had always thought the stories could be made into a beautiful series of animated movies. We weren't a television family, but were excited about this opportunity to expand our audience beyond the Texas Panhandle. I signed the contract. Unfortunately, it didn't give me any creative control.

The program aired in May 1985, and CBS did a nice job with the animation, voices, and the character designs. But after watching it several times, we noticed that they had removed the family from the story. Sally May had become the ranch boss, not Loper's wife, and there were no children.

We were puzzled. Why did they do that? We could only conclude that someone at the network didn't consider the family as important as we did. They used my innocent little story to make a political statement, and did it without consulting me.

In 1986, we got a call from Disney Studios about movie rights. I flew out to California and spent four days touring the studio and talking with executives and animators. I met Roy Disney, Jr. and spent time with animators. They liked the Hank stories and I was thrilled, naturally. As a kid, I had watched all the classic Disney movies at the Ellis Theater in Perryton, and watched them again with our children on VCR at home. I couldn't think of a better home for the Hank stories than Disney.

But then we got the contract, a 32-page document that required me to give up all rights to all stories and characters, "in all languages, known and unknown, in all parts of the universe." It offered no royalties to me, the guy who invented Hank.

My father, who had read a lot of contracts in his real estate business, blew a gasket. "You can't sign this thing!" Gary Rinker and I had come to the same conclusion. We tried to negotiate a better contract with the lawyers, but that didn't go anywhere. I didn't sign the contract. I would have been signing away my life's work.

In the late 1990s, we tried again, this time with Nickelodeon. We were able to negotiate a contract for a feature-length animated movie and began the development process. I wrote a screenplay and Nickelodeon hired another writer to revise it. He completely rewrote my script and turned my story into a gender war, females against males. The project came to a sad end. We never made the movie, but we got the rights back.

Over the years, Gary has talked with dozens of companies and individuals who were interested in the movie and television rights, some established companies in the entertainment business, others just fly-by-night speculators. One fellow, we learned later, had actually talked to Willie Nelson about doing Hank's voice in a movie, and they shopped it around to studios in California. The problem was that the guy had no contract with us and no authority to do anything.

In 2015, Gary, Mark, and I decided to form our own company, HTC Productions, and try to make a television series as an independent venture. Mark and I wrote ten thirty-minute scripts for television. We found investors for the development phase and worked with an animation group in New Zealand to produce an eleven-minute pilot episode and a "pitch pack." The pitch pack was a promotional device we gave to distributors and investors, a full-color book that showed character designs and landscapes, and described the entire project.

Mark and Ralph Boral took the material to the Cannes Film Festival and showed it to distributors.

Gary and Kim Rinker, 2018. Photo by Kris Erickson

Mark Erickson - Photo by Kris Erickson

Several companies expressed an interest, but for one reason or another, nothing ever came of it. Many of those companies thought our story and animation style were too "retro," old-fashioned. To them, our pilot film lacked the noise and flash of modern animation, and they were right. *We wanted it that way!* We weren't trying to make a gaudy splash of animated fireworks. We wanted to tell a good old-fashioned story with interesting characters that would give three generations of viewers the gift of innocent laughter.

Years ago, some guy in California summed it up by saying, "Story is EVERYTHING." That was Walt Disney, and he did pretty well following that concept.

As I write this (July 2018), we have signed a contract with an established Texas film director who discovered Hank in the best possible way, reading *Lost In the Dark Unchanted Forest* to his five-year old son. They laughed together and loved the story, and that love showed up in the screenplay he wrote. It's warm, funny, faithful to the spirit of the Hank stories, and respectful to our audience, the people who "brung us to the dance."

Now we are moving forward in the development process, which includes lining up major voice talent, working up character designs, selecting an animation company, and shopping the project to distributors and investors. Maybe we'll get bucked off again, but maybe we won't. If we get it done, we will produce a feature-length, theater-release animated movie that will make you proud.

What we are trying to do—maintain creative control of the Hank franchise in a complex business environment—is very difficult, but we plan to do it right. What would be the point of doing it wrong? With all the problems this world is facing—diplomatic, political, economic, and spiritual—all of us need some good, honest, innocent laughter.

Are you famous? Rich?

At this point in our history, Americans are awash in "stars" and celebrities, some of whom haven't really done much and are famous for being famous. I try to keep some perspective on my place in this world. I recall the words of Isaiah: "All men are like grass and all their glory is like the flowers of the field."

I find it helpful to compare my accomplishments to those of J.S. Bach, Shakespeare, and Abraham Lincoln, not to some author who is topping the New York Times bestseller list or to a singer who has a huge following on Twitter.

If you compare yourself to Bach, you can't escape humility, because the man was a genius of breathtaking proportions. Did Bach consider himself rich and famous? I doubt that he ever had time to think about it. He was too busy composing music for the Lutheran church that paid his salary, and trying to put food on the table for his big family.

I am Kris's husband and the father of our three children, a citizen of a little town in Texas, and a member of the church choir. I go to my office every morning, do honest work, and try to produce stories that will make readers better than they were before.

I'm famous enough to get fan mail from kids who say, "I love your books," and sometimes people come up to me in the Amarillo airport and thank me for giving their children something decent to read. That's famous enough for me.

Am I rich? Hank has been a good dog and has brought me a comfortable standard of living, and I feel blessed for that. But what makes me rich is that I've been married to the same lady for fifty years, I've got three children and two dogs who like me, I have a clear conscience, and I sleep well at night.

I'm doing what I want to do and I find meaning in it. Could a billion dollars bring something better than that? I doubt it.

What advice do you have for writers?

Sometimes, when I'm asked this question, I say, "Marry for money! It will be a big help in your writing career." That is a humorous answer, of course, and I don't recommend it. Here are a few reasonable suggestions:

- Writers learn to write by writing—not by reading books or taking courses or talking, but by writing.
- Write about something you know and care about.
- Turn off your screens. Read, live, observe, and love.
- Write in a disciplined manner, even if it's only 30 minutes a day.
- Seek light, not darkness. Seek wisdom, beauty, honesty, and meaning.
- Make your readers better than they were before. If you can't do that, what's the point?
- Diagram sentences in your mind: subject | verb \ object.
- Try to avoid using adverbs. They're weak.
- Don't write anything that would shame your mother.
- Read my book *Story Craft*. It gives my best advice to writers.

JRE speaking to Nathan Dahlstrom's creative writing class in Lubbock. Photo by Nathan Dahlstrom.

How long will you go on writing Hank?

The book of Ecclesiastes says, "Man knoweth not his time." We don't know how much time we have on this earth or how many books we will end up writing.

When I wrote the first Hank book, I didn't expect to write a second one. When I did, I never thought it would become a series, and I never would have dreamed that by 2019, we would have 74 of them.

I continue to enjoy writing these stories. I am fascinated by Hank's quirky personality and find him endlessly fascinating. If the time ever comes when I dread writing the stories, I will probably retire, because if they're not fun for me, you won't like them either.

But we're not there yet and I can tell you that the next six books are already written. I hope they bless your life.

Erickson interviewing Erickson in 1978. Photo and trickery by Kris Erickson.

Photo by John Weast for The National Ranching Heritage Center.

Appendix: Erickson's Non-Hank Books

Through Time and the Valley (1978). Shoal Creek Publishers, Maverick Books, and University of North Texas Press. Photographs by Bill Ellzey.

Panhandle Cowboy (1980). With a preface by Larry McMurtry. University of Nebraska Press and University of North Texas Press. Photographs by Bill Ellzey.

The Modern Cowboy (1981). University of Nebraska Press and University of North Texas Press. Photographs by Kris Erickson.

The Devil in Texas and Other Cowboy Tales (1982). Maverick Books and Gulf Publishing Company. Illustrations are by Gerald L. Holmes.

Cowboys Are Partly Human (1983). Maverick Books and Gulf Publishing Company. Illustrations by Gerald L. Holmes.

Alkali County Tales (1984). Maverick Books and Gulf Publishing Company. Illustrations by Gerald L. Holmes.

ReAnna Wilson helping with a branding. Photo by Kris Erickson.

The Hunter (1984). Doubleday and Company.

Ace Reid: Cowpoke (1984). Maverick Books.

Essays on Writing and Publishing (1985). Maverick Books.

Cowboys Are a Separate Species (1986). Maverick Books and Gulf Publishing Company. Illustrations by Gerald L. Holmes.

Cowboys Are Old Enough To Know Better (1986). Maverick Books and Gulf Publishing Company. Illustrations by Gerald L. Holmes.

Cowboy Country (1986). Maverick Books. Photographs by Kris Erickson.

Catch Rope—The Long Arm of the Cowboy (1994). University of North Texas Press. Photographs by Kris Erickson.

LZ Cowboy: A Cowboy's Journal 1979-81 (2001). University of North Texas Press. Photographs by Kris Erickson.

Some Babies Grow Up To Be Cowboys: A Collection of Articles and Essays (1999). University of North Texas Press. Photographs by Kris Erickson.

Cowboy Fiddler (1992). With Frankie McWhorter. Texas Tech Press and University of North Texas Press. Photographs by Kris Erickson, others courtesy of Frankie McWhorter.

Horse Fixin': Forty Years of Working With Problem Horses (1992). With Frankie McWhorter. Texas Tech Press.

Friends: Cowboys, Cattle, Horses, Dogs, Cats, and Coons (2002). University of North Texas Press. Photographs by Kris Erickson.

Prairie Gothic: The Story of a West Texas Family (2005). Foreword by Elmer Kelton. University of North Texas Press.

Moonshiner's Gold (2005). Viking-Penguin and Maverick Books.

Discovery At Flint Springs (2007). Viking Press and Maverick Books.

Story Craft: Reflections on Faith, Culture, and Writing (2009). Introduction by Gene Edward Veith and foreword by Nancy Pearcey. Maverick Books.

Fear's Return (2011). Maverick Books.

Photo by Nathan Dahlstrom

Index

JRE's award from the Texas Literary Hall of Fame, 2019

John Erickson and family and friends at the "Texas Literary Hall of Fame" Induction Ceremony, 2019

JRE and Dixie, Photo by Nathan Dahlstrom